AMERICAN HORTICULTURAL SOCIETY
PRACTICAL GUIDES

FLOWERING
SHRUBS

AMERICAN HORTICULTURAL SOCIETY
PRACTICAL GUIDES

FLOWERING SHRUBS

CHARLES CHESSHIRE

DK PUBLISHING, INC.
www.dk.com.

A DK PUBLISHING BOOK
www.dk.com

SERIES EDITOR Pamela Brown
SERIES ART EDITOR Stephen Josland
ART EDITOR Rachael Parfitt

MANAGING EDITOR Louise Abbott
MANAGING ART EDITOR Lee Griffiths
US EDITOR Ray Rogers

DTP DESIGNER Matthew Greenfield

PRODUCTION Ruth Charlton, Mandy Innes

First American Edition, 1999
2 4 6 8 10 9 7 5 3

Published in the United States by
DK Publishing, Inc., 95 Madison Avenue, New York, New York 10016

Copyright © 1999
Dorling Kindersley Limited, London

Library of Congress Cataloging-in-Publication data

Flowering shrubs.
        p.   cm.   -- (AHS practical guides)
      Includes index.
      ISBN 0-7894-4157-8 (alk. paper)
      1. Flowering shrubs   I. DK Publishing, Inc.   II. Series.
SB435.F644 1999
635.9'76--dc21   98-48212
                                          CIP
Reproduced by Colourscan, Singapore
Printed and bound by Star Standard Industries, Singapore

CONTENTS

SHRUBS IN THE GARDEN 7

How to use shrubs in every style of garden
to add structure, interest, and beautiful flowering
displays to any planting.

LOOKING AFTER SHRUBS 27

How to plant and care for shrubs so that they give their
best display; pruning demystified.

RECOMMENDED FLOWERING SHRUBS 38

The best shrubs to choose and grow for year-round
interest in any garden or situation.

SHRUBS IN THE GARDEN

WHAT IS A SHRUB?

SHRUBS ARE BUSHY PLANTS whose stems become woody with age, enabling them to survive winter weather and grow and flower for many years. Their lifespan varies from a few years to many decades, but in a garden context they are valued for the lasting beauty that they bring to many plantings. There are many shrubs with lovely foliage, but the majority of garden favorites are chosen chiefly for their flowering displays.

WHY SHRUBS FLOWER

Shrubs flower to reproduce themselves, the blooms attracting pollinating insects that enable them to set seed. Most bear male and female flowers on the same plant, either fertilizing themselves or each other as insects move from flower to flower. Rarely, as with *Skimmia*, male and female flowers are borne on separate plants and you need to grow both for a good display, but even with these, plant breeding has produced types that flower well alone.

WHY CHOOSE SHRUBS?

- Long-lasting and bring structure and interest to plantings year after year.
- Huge range of sizes, habits, flower color, and foliage interest from which to choose.
- Low-maintenance compared to other plant groups; most stand up well to bad weather.
- No nurturing of young plants or raising from seed is necessary.
- Flowering and fruiting shrubs attract wildlife, providing food and nesting sites.

EASY-CARE DISPLAYS
From the earliest flowers on bare spring branches, as with forsythia (left), to the richness of summer blooms such as buddleia (far left) and hibiscus (facing page), flowering shrubs bring color and beauty to the garden through the seasons. Many, including the ones pictured here, are easy to grow and, once established, virtually look after themselves; some, such as the hibiscus, do not even need annual pruning.

BUDDLEJA DAVIDII 'FASCINATING'   *FORSYTHIA* 'ARNOLD GIANT'

◀ *HIBISCUS SYRIACUS* 'BLUE BIRD' *A showy shrub for full sun that flowers in summer.*

SHRUBS IN PLANTING PLANS

It would be a poor garden that did not include any flowering shrubs. They have become increasingly popular because, in general, they require less maintenance than herbaceous plants, which die down in winter, and bedding, which must be regularly renewed. They form a year-round background for many plantings, important in the present day when gardens are smaller and plantings are more constantly in view. In fact, the traditional herbaceous border has largely disappeared in favor

> It would be difficult to design a satisfying garden without shrubs

of the mixed border, where shrubs and woody climbers lend height, structure, and winter interest to plantings of annuals and perennials. Mixed borders may be planned to associate and contrast textures and colors across the different plant groups or to give carefully paced flowering displays

▲ SEASONAL CHEER
Shrubs (here a forsythia) can add lasting, year-round interest near the house; even where there is no soil, many grow happily in pots.

▼ FORM AND STRUCTURE
Berberis × stenophylla *makes an excellent hedge, but growing it as a specimen shrub (as here) lets it develop its lovely, arching habit.*

◄ CITY CHOICE
As well as being good container plants, hydrangeas can also grow in both sun and shade and have a useful, long flowering season in summer.

▼ SETTING THE SCENE
Rhododendrons are perfect plants for acidic soils under trees and in woodland areas, and they associate naturally and beautifully with shade-loving perennials.

throughout the year so that there is always something to admire, even in the deepest and darkest part of winter.

Some flowering shrubs, such as magnolias, can make spectacular specimen plants to be admired year-round, even for elegant bare branch structure, while others such as forsythia and spirea, although having lovely flowers, have very dull foliage and form rather uninteresting mounds of greenery for the rest of the season; these are best merged with other shrubs and perennials that flower at a different time.

Mass plantings of one kind of shrub can make for bold effects, and many can be useful for covering the ground, such as evergreen azaleas, cotoneasters, *Hebe*, *Hypericum*, viburnums, and *Skimmia*. This characteristic is often exploited for large public spaces but may be less appropriate for the small garden, since many of these plants are dull out of flower.

A number of flowering shrubs make good hedges, adding color, light, and fragrance to boundaries. While many flower better grown informally, some, including thorny barberries and firethorns, can be lightly clipped to form densely growing barriers.

YEAR-ROUND INTEREST

With careful planning and taking care to choose plants that are suited by the conditions your garden offers (climate, soil type, and sun or shade), you can have shrubs blooming nearly year-round, with the scarcer autumn- and winter-flowerers supplemented by the fruits and berries of many that flowered earlier in the season. Don't forget the value of foliage, too; fresh spring leaves, the rich autumn tints of some deciduous shrubs, and the year-round elegance of glossy evergreens.

THE FIRST FLOWERS

In late winter and very early spring, *Chimonanthus* (wintersweet) and *Hamamelis* (witch hazel) produce small flowers, yet because they are borne on bare stems they show off to great advantage; moreover, both are intensely fragrant, and their scent may be detected even before the shrub comes into view. Don't plant these shrubs too far away from the house, where they may not be visited in cold weather.

Both *Hamamelis* and *Chimonanthus* grow equally well in full sun and in the shade of a woodland garden. In cold climates, the protection from overhead trees will help prevent damage to early-flowering shrubs from frost or cold wind. Such conditions, where the soil is acidic,

enable you to grow camellias, azaleas, and rhododendrons, giving a wonderful display from early spring into early summer. They have the advantage of being evergreen, providing a solid background for their showy flowers. They could in turn be

---

Intense fragrance is a feature of many early-flowering shrubs

---

underplanted with varieties of *Sarcococca*, which also flower early. Camellias start flowering in autumn and continue into the spring, depending on the region and the weather.

▲ *CHIMONANTHUS PRAECOX*
The small, waxy flowers of wintersweet are heavily fragrant, but the shrub needs a protected position.

▲ *CYTISUS* 'WINDLESHAM RUBY'
Brooms are cheerful spring shrubs for full sun that grow fast but do not live long.

▲ *SYRINGA VULGARIS*
Lilacs (this is 'Sensation') are popular fragrant shrubs for spring that need plenty of space to develop.

◄ SPRING FRESHNESS
'The Bride' is one of
the finest forms of
Exochorda. It is
compact and spring-
flowering, the whole
plant being smothered
in bloom. It thrives in
any soil type in full
sun or in partial shade.

▼ SUMMER RICHNESS
The deep purple
flowers of Lespedeza
in late summer make
a good contrast
with Hydrangea
paniculata (see p.42).
It should be pruned
hard in late winter
to encourage long,
arching shoots.

In more alkaline soils there are small,
shrubby types of *Prunus* that flower in
pink or white on bare wood in early
spring, such as *Prunus cerasifera* and
P. × cistena, both of which have dark
purple-leaved forms. *Chaenomeles* – the
flowering quinces, or japonicas – with bright
red, pink, and white flowers held tightly
against the old wood look good growing
as freestanding shrubs (up to 8ft/2.5m tall)
or tied in and clipped flat against a wall.
These and *Mahonia japonica* will grow in
almost any soil, the latter bearing robust,
fragrant spikes of yellow flowers above
bold whorls of evergreen leaves.

Forsythias and *Ribes* (flowering currants)
both flower around this time and look
delightful with an underplanting of early
spring bulbs in bloom. Some people dislike
forsythias for the very reason that others
love them: their brilliant splash of yellow
flowers, unrelieved by green leaves. The
pungent aroma of some currants, especially
R. sanguineum, can be a drawback.

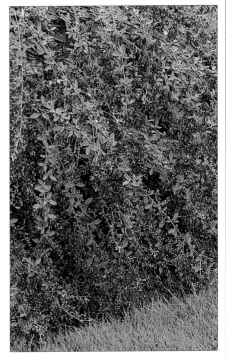

THE START OF SUMMER

In late spring *Ceanothus*, *Exochorda*, *Cytisus*, and the heavily fragrant *Viburnum carlesii* and *V. × burkwoodii* will thrive in most soil types, and as summer begins, other fragrant shrubs such as mock oranges and lilacs begin flowering. Other fine shrubs for the turn of the seasons include *Kolkwitzia*, *Deutzia*, *Cistus*, *Buddleja alternifolia*, and *Escallonia*, perhaps underplanted with *Helianthemum*.

As the heat of summer arrives, *Abelia*, *Hypericum*, and *Potentilla* can fill in between larger shrubs. Shrubs that thrive in dry soil (*see pp.70–73*) are a boon in the summer garden, whatever the soil type. Hydrangeas are valuable at this time of year. The lacecaps are best for light shade, especially under trees, while the mophead hortensias are excellent container plants. The larger and very reliable *H. paniculata* has cones of white florets that fade to pink. It is best in full sun, where it would look

▲ LATE BLOOMERS
Gray-leaved shrubs that are pruned hard in spring, such as Caryopteris (*'Ferndown', above*) *and* Perovskia, *will reward the wait while their stems grow back throughout summer with valuable late flowering displays.*

◀ SECOND SHOW
Flowering shrubs that bear bright berries and fruits, such as this Cotoneaster salicifolius *'Exburyensis', double their value in the garden with a renewed season of interest in autumn.*

good with *Vitex* and *Lespedeza*, both with purple flowers. Two stalwarts for full sun are the butterfly bush, *Buddleja davidii* and its many varieties, and *Hibiscus syriacus*. Both flower well into late summer. *Perovskia* and *Caryopteris* are also ideal for the sunny garden, together with hardy fuchsias and lavender. In a warm year, late summer-bloomers will continue their show into autumn, when flowers may be scarce. Other flowering shrubs may have new autumn attractions: the beautiful berries of cotoneasters and flame-colored leaves of *Cotinus* (smoke bush), for example.

PLANNING WITH COLOR

It's not difficult to choose shrubs that will carry a color theme year-round, or to vary the palette through the seasons to suit other plants (*see next page*) coming into bloom. Whites, pinks, and yellows tend to predominate among spring-flowering shrubs, while richer, duskier hues are more the preserve of those that bloom in summer, but there are many exceptions to the rule. Shrubs with white flowers (*see below*) provide an attractive but neutral foil for almost any color scheme.

MAHONIA × MEDIA 'CHARITY'
Some Mahonia *flower in autumn, others in spring. Autumn-bloomers such as 'Charity' can sometimes flower right through winter until spring-flowerers begin their display.*

WHITE-FLOWERED SHRUBS

FOR WINTER-SPRING

Azaleas *Rhododendron* 'Delaware Valley White', *R. arborescens*.
Camellia Look for *C. japonica* 'Alba Plena' or 'Mathotiana Alba', or 'Nuccio's Gem'.
Chaenomeles speciosa 'Nivalis' Flowers on bare stems.
Daphne mezereum f. alba Fragrant.
Erica carnea Groundcover for acidic soil; choose 'Springwood White' or 'Snow Queen'
Exochorda × macrantha 'The Bride' Appears almost completely white when in full flower.
Magnolia stellata 'Waterlily' Fragrant.
Rhododendron hybrids Evergreens for acidic soil; 'Cunningham's White', 'Dora Amateis', 'Loder's White', and 'Mrs. P.D. Williams' are all tough and reliable.
Viburnum Many with the bonus of fragrance.

FOR SUMMER-AUTUMN

Clethra alnifolia Fragrant, for acidic soils.
Deutzia gracilis Looks marvelous with roses.
Hibiscus syriacus 'Diana' (*see p.41*)
Hydrangea paniculata, H. arborescens, H. quercifolia, H. macrophylla 'Lanarth White' and 'Madame Emile Mouillière' Mainstays for the summer garden.
Lavandula angustifolia 'Nana Alba' A small lavender for fragrant edging.
Philadelphus Clusters of small flowers, intensely fragrant.
Potentilla 'McKay's White'.
Rosa Many to choose from.
Syringa Fragrant panicles in many colors; 'Miss Ellen Wilmott', 'Madame Lemoine', 'Mont Blanc', and 'Jan van Tol' are white.
Weigela 'Candida'.

SHRUBS WITH OTHER PLANTS

ALTHOUGH SHRUBS ARE OFTEN grown exclusively with other shrubs, it is usually far more interesting to grow them in combination with other plants, including bulbs, herbaceous perennials, annuals, groundcovers, and climbers. Equally, in a herbaceous planting, shrubs can be used to add height, weight, and a longer season to what is often only a brief spring or summer display.

UNDER- AND INTERPLANTING

Bulbs are perhaps the easiest of the other plant groups to add under shrub plantings because many can be left undisturbed and unattended for years. (This is the type of bulb planting known as "naturalized": they will spread and form colonies of their own accord.) The bulbs often flower in the spring, benefiting from light before the leaves of the shrub have unfolded. As their foliage dies away, the burgeoning shrubs cover the unsightliness. Among herbaceous perennials, there are many that can cover ground beneath shrubs with the minimum of care: choose those that have attractive flowers and persistently attractive foliage. For the gaps between shrubs, you can choose low-maintenance perennials that complement the easy-care advantages of shrubs. Don't confine interplanting to low-growing plants: flower spikes and spires, such as foxgloves and *Verbascum*, will add surprise vertical contrasts and often self-seed to spring up randomly each year.

▲ SOFT COLORS
This Lavatera *is flattered by* Acer negundo *'Flamingo', a foliage shrub, and an underplanting of hardy perennial* Geranium. *This is a combination with a long season.*

▶ EXTROVERT PLANTING
The purple foliage of the Cotinus *is in dark contrast to the yellows of the* Genista *behind and the* Kniphofia *in the foreground: a group for the adventurous gardener.*

◄ UNDERPLANTING
*In late winter,
snowdrops bloom in
the light that falls
between the flower-
studded branches of*
Hamamelis ×
intermedia *'Pallida'.*

▼ SHADY LAYERS
The pink buds of
Viburnum davidii
*break between a
flowering* Euphorbia
*and a background
of variegated holly
in this layered
planting design.*

CAREFUL COMBINATIONS

Some roses associate beautifully with other flowering shrubs although they do require a little more care. Spring-flowering shrubs mix extremely well with early species roses, and as the shrub rose season gets under way, fragrant shrubs such as mock oranges and lilacs produce a lovely, cottagey, summery feel. There are climbers that can be allowed to twine into shrubs as host supports; those that die down in winter or are cut back in spring will simplify pruning.

PLANT PARTNERS

Bulbs for underplanting: *Chionodoxa,* daffodils (many small types naturalize well), *Scilla,* snowdrops (*Galanthus*), woodland anemones (*Anemone nemorosa, A. sylvestris*).

Underplanting with a long season: Astilbes, columbines, *Epimedium,* ferns, *Geranium,* hostas, *Persicaria,* and *Thalictrum.*

Easy-care interplanting: *Alchemilla,* asters, daylilies (*Hemerocallis*), irises, *Nepeta,* peonies, and *Rudbeckia.*

Vertical accents: Foxgloves (*Digitalis*) and lilies for shade, *Veronicastrum virginicum* and *Verbascum* for sun.

Climbers to scramble into shrubs: Clematis: large-flowered hybrids, or the *C. viticella* types, pruned hard in late winter; perennial peas (*Lathyrus*) for large shrubs and sweet peas for small ones; *Tropaeolum speciosum.*

WORKING WITH THE SOIL

THERE ARE MANY SHRUBS that are remarkably unfussy as to the kinds of soil they grow in, but there are also a number, including some very desirable plants, that have strict preferences. If these requirements are ignored, the shrubs will suffer, fail to grow, and may even die. The primary considerations are for the texture, moisture, and nutrient content of the soil, and for its acidity and alkalinity – known as its pH value.

STRUCTURE AND TEXTURE

Soil type ranges between two extremes, heavy clay and sand. Clay soil can be molded in your hand when saturated with water, while sandy soil is light, dry, and gritty-textured. If your soil seems to fall between these two types, then you are fortunate: many shrubs will be happy in your garden. If it tends toward one extreme, choice will be more restricted.

Heavy clay soils have a naturally high level of nutrients but retain water, so avoid planting shrubs that like dry conditions. Plant roots take longer to penetrate clay, so lighten it by adding organic matter upon planting. Ground that tends to become waterlogged at certain times of the year will kill many shrubs, especially evergreens. Some plants, such as some *Clethra*, tolerate and even benefit from occasional flooding. Sandy soils are easier to work but are free-draining and often low in nutrients, so add well-rotted manure as well other organic

> ## Waterlogging makes some shrubs die; others can take some flooding

matter, except for plants that prefer poor soils such as *Cytisus, Genista,* and *Tamarix*. In very poor soils laden with construction rubble, buddleias will thrive.

CHANGING COLORS
If the soil is too limy, blue-flowered hydrangeas turn pink. On slightly limy soils they can be encouraged to retain their color by adding iron sulfate and feeding well – but choosing other blue-flowered shrubs is a much easier option.

PIERIS 'FOREST FLAME'
Pieris *belong to the same family as rhododendrons and, like them, they prefer an acidic soil. This one has brilliant red young growth and carries erect then pendent clusters of white flowers in spring.*

PHILADELPHUS 'BELLE ETOILE'
A very reliable shrub with one of the strongest perfumes of any plant. Most mock oranges will grow on almost any soil, acidic or alkaline, that is fertile and well drained.

ACIDIC OR ALKALINE?

The pH of your soil is easy to test with simple kits available at most garden centers. Plants that prefer acidic soil include rhododendrons and azaleas, *Pieris*, camellias, *Kalmia* (mountain laurel), and heaths and heathers. If the pH is too high for these plants, their leaves turn yellow and they may die. It is difficult to make an alkaline soil acidic, so if you do have limy soil it is best not to try to grow this group of plants. However, if you have slightly acidic soil, you may find that many of the plants that ideally prefer alkaline soils will grow perfectly well. Some gardeners add garden lime to acidic soil to increase its pH for the benefit of plants such as roses and Mediterranean shrubs, lavender and *Santolina*, for example.

ALKALINE SOILS

Alkaline soil does not pose nearly so many problems as acidic soil *(see pp.56–59 for suitable plants)*, but if your garden is on limestone, try the following shrubs. Many of them are equally happy in neutral to acidic soil.

Berberis	*Philadelphus*
Buddleja	*Potentilla*
Cistus	*Prunus*
Cotoneaster	*Rosmarinus*
Deutzia	*Santolina*
Escallonia	*Sarcococca*
Forsythia	*Syringa*
Hydrangea villosa	*Viburnum*
(not other species)	*Weigela*
Kolkwitzia	
Osmanthus	
Paeonia (tree peonies)	

SUN AND SHADE

AN IMPORTANT FACTOR TO take into consideration before planting is what level of sun or shade a shrub prefers. This can also depend on the part of the world you are in. In Maine, where summers are normally cool and the intensity of the sun is relatively weak, many shade-loving plants are quite happy in full sun. Conversely, in Georgia, where the summer sun is harsh and intense, many sun-loving shrubs may prefer to be, and grow happily in, some shade.

ASSESSING YOUR SITE

The degree of shade is crucial when choosing shrubs for your site. Deep shade (*see facing page*) is the most restrictive of choice, but part-day or light shade may deny you only the most committed sun-loving plants. However, although many shrubs will grow in shade, they may flower less than in sun. There are also different kinds of shade. The shade on the dark side of a building is deeper and more consistent than the shade cast by a tree. The shade under trees also varies and affects the quality of the soil beneath.

> ### Dry soil can be a challenge in both sunny and shady sites

Camellias and rhododendrons will grow well under the dappled shade of deep-rooting oaks or tulip trees, for instance, the annual leaf-fall enriching the soil to help them thrive. Shallow-rooting trees and conifers will not only shade the ground beneath but also deprive any shrubs of moisture and nutrition. Shrubs planted in such conditions may require additional irrigation and mulching with leafmold or compost.

Growing shrubs in full sun can also be variable. Buildings that are in full sun can reflect light and heat, especially if painted white, so that nearby plants with sensitive foliage will actually scorch in hotter climates. Plants grown on a south-facing bank not only receive a lot of light but also experience much more heat and dryness at the roots. In such harsh conditions there are plants such as *Abutilon*, *Cistus*, *Cytisus*, *Grevillea*, *Rosmarinus*, and *Yucca*, native to dry regions such as Australia, South Africa, or the Mediterranean, that would be ideal. In dry spells, these plants will still need watering until they are established.

YUCCA RECURVIFOLIA
Yuccas are not only suitable for full sun but also tolerate very dry situations, where they will be more likely to flower well. Yuccas provide a bold and striking accent in the border.

THE FOLIAGE FACTOR

Some variegated shrubs, especially shrubs with golden foliage such as *Philadelphus coronarius* 'Aureus' and *Sambucus racemosa* 'Sutherland Gold', whose parent species are happy in full sun, will scorch in hot sun. If grown in deep shade, however, the same foliage will lose its color intensity. Getting light levels right lets you enjoy the full beauty of flower and foliage contrasts.

▲ FLASH OF AZALEAS
If grown in deep shade, azaleas will not flower well, but in dappled woodland, as here, the conditions are ideal and the flowers will last longer.

▼ *FATSIA JAPONICA*
Grown chiefly for its handsome, bold leaves, this plant, like its close relatives the ivies, will grow in deep shade and once established will tolerate quite dry soil.

PLANTS FOR DEEP SHADE

Camellia japonica
Daphne laureola
Elaeagnus × *ebbingei*
Fatsia japonica
Hypericum calycinum
Mahonia aquifolium
Nandina domestica
Osmanthus heterophyllus
Rhododendron, many
Sarcococca
Skimmia
Vinca minor (Periwinkle)

For details of these plants and others, see *Recommended Flowering Shrubs*, pp.64–65.

SHRUBS FOR WALLS

ALTHOUGH CLIMBERS are more associated with growing on walls, shrubs can give more substance and year-round interest. Garden and house walls are ideal sites for certain shrubs that are either too sensitive to cold for the rest of the garden or whose flexible stems benefit from support. These wall shrubs can also be used as supports for other climbers, such as clematis, to twine through.

SUITABLE SHRUBS

Shrubs can both enhance and camouflage vertical surfaces, whether simply grown alongside garden boundaries and buildings to break up straight lines, or trained (either loosely or more formally) against walls and fences. You must choose shrubs carefully if you intend to tie them in. Many shrubs with a floppy or scrambling habit look neater and gain more height if main stems are loosely tied in against a support, but not all are suitable. Relatively few shrubs tolerate the manipulation and pruning necesary for formal fan- or espalier-training and still grow and flower well. (*See* Recommended Flowering Shrubs, *pp.60–63*, for some suitable choices.) You must also ensure that the wall or fence can support both the weight of the shrub and its supports, such as a trellis or wires.

CALLISTEMON RIGIDUS
Native to Australia, Callistemon *relish hot and dry conditions. They have showy, fluffy flower spikes that give them their common name, bottlebrush. They lend themselves to growing against walls, either as free-standing shrubs or informally but carefully tied in.*

WALL-TRAINED
PYRACANTHA
*Firethorns (here
P.'Watereri') can be
clipped to within
12in/30cm of a wall
and are suitable for
shady areas. Their
clusters of small white
flowers are followed
by bunches of red,
orange, or yellow
berries, according to
the variety. Firethorns
can be clipped tightly
enough to frame
windows and doors
attractively. Prune
them in midsummer
and in late winter.*

CHALLENGING YOUR CLIMATE

You may find that a wall or fence provides a useful microclimate that will allow you to grow shrubs that would otherwise perish exposed in the open garden. A blanket of horticultural fleece or dry mulch of straw at the base can help get such plants through the winter in borderline areas or if the weather becomes unusually cold. Walls may not only give shelter from cold winds

> Not all walls provide shelter: some are cold and windy

but also hold and reflect heat, encouraging some shrubs to flower more profusely. However, not all vertical surfaces are "warm"; it depends on exposure and on how much sun is received and at what time of day, so check this out before choosing a shrub. Check also whether (as often happens with north- and south-facing walls) there are cross-winds that could buffet plants. "Cold" walls, however, need

not be problematic. A warm wall that is in sun from midday onward may be perfect for some warm-climate plants – *Abutilon, Ceanothus, Carpenteria,* and *Fremontodendron* – but too intensely hot, say, for a camellia. Camellias need some shelter, however. Firethorns, flowering quinces, and cotoneasters are good, tough choices for a cold or windy wall.

PLANTING DISTANCES

It is important to decide whether you are simply going to grow a shrub freestanding in the shelter of the wall, or actually tie it in: this will affect where you plant it. Even shrubs that are going to be trained in (*see p.36*) need to be planted some distance from the wall, especially those that get top-heavy but dislike too much pruning, such as evergreen *Ceanothus.* This will also lessen the effects of "rain shadow" at the wall's base, where the soil can get very dry, particularly where eaves and gutters overhang.

Rain shadow can be used to advantage in wet areas if you want to grow shrubs that like arid spots, such as *Callistemon,* but in other cases, improve the moisture-retentiveness of the soil before planting (*see p.28*), and make sure the shrubs get enough water.

SHRUBS FOR FRAGRANCE

THE MOST PRECIOUS QUALITY A plant can have apart from color is fragrance. Indeed, there are many shrubs that have fairly insignificant flowers but whose fragrance makes them worthy of inclusion in any garden. Other than its obvious appeal to us, fragrance is designed to attract pollinating insects, so scented flowers will lure visitors both pretty and useful to the garden. Fragrance is also essential in gardens designed and planted for the visually impaired.

SHRUBS WITH SWEET SCENTS

Plant fragrant shrubs near doors, patios, and paths, but use them in out-of-the-way corners, too, to surprise the senses. There is a mysterious, even elusive quality to some scents: the small evergreen *Sarcococca*, or Christmas box, has a fragrance that can carry for extraordinary distances despite its diminutive size.

Use fragrant shrubs, also, to attract wildlife into your garden. The few late winter- and early spring-blooming shrubs such as *Mahonia*, *Hamamelis*, and viburnums often have powerfully perfumed flowers to attract the few early flying insects that are about, but by late spring and summer, shrubs unleash a host of scents into the garden to vie for the

FRAGRANT FLOWERS FOR WILDLIFE
Buddleja davidii *is well-named the "butterfly bush." Butterflies love the purple flowers of the common lavender form, but this white-flowered variety attracts them, too.*

> ## Lure butterflies in search of nectar with scented flowers

pollinators' attentions. Use them to create havens of fragrance to enhance summer days and evenings: many scents intensify when the weather is warm and slightly humid and often persist into dusk. A pot of lavender by a path or seating area, buzzing with bees, is for many people the epitome of summer sensations. The heat bounced back by paving and gravel heightens the aromatic qualities of sun-loving shrubs such as lavender, rosemary, and *Cistus ladanifer*, all of which have scented foliage, too.

◄ *MAHONIA ×
MEDIA* 'UNDERWAY'
*The bright, honey-
scented flowers of*
Mahonia *are a treat
when summer is far
away: there are kinds
that flower at both
ends of the winter
season.*

▼ *DAPHNE ×
BURKWOODII
Daphnes are not
the easiest of
shrubs to grow (this
is one of the least
temperamental), but
if you can make
them thrive in your
garden, you will be
rewarded by one of
the most exquisite
flower scents.*

TOP SHRUBS FOR SCENT

LATE WINTER AND SPRING
Chimonanthus praecox (wintersweet)
Daphne
Hamamelis
Lonicera (honeysuckle), such as
  L. fragrantissima
Osmanthus
Prunus mume
Rhododendron
Sarcococca
Viburnum × *burkwoodii* and other viburnums

SUMMER AND AUTUMN
Abelia × *grandiflora*
Buddleja (butterfly bush)
Choisya ternata (Mexican orange blossom)
Elaeagnus angustifolia, E. pungens
Lavandula (lavenders)
Philadelphus (mock orange)
Rosa (roses)
Syringa (lilac)

For details of these shrubs and others, see
Recommended Flowering Shrubs, pp.52–55.

EXPOSED AND WINDY SITES

A N EXPOSED GARDEN, OR PART OF A GARDEN, may offer inhospitable conditions to plants, leaving them open to cold, drying winds and frost or, in coastal regions, to salt-laden winds and storms. Such conditions may not only damage vulnerable plants but also distort their growth. You can, however, choose shrubs that will stand up well, avoiding those native to sheltered woodland, for example, and selecting those that have adapted themselves to blustery climates.

NATURAL ADAPTATION

Generally, plants that are naturally equipped to withstand drying winds tend to have small leaves. Gray or silver leaves, often with the stems and foliage covered in fine hairs, also often indicate suitable plants, as does succulent growth, in which water reserves are guarded by thick, tough leaf and stem surfaces.

In moderately windy gardens, tough, durable shrubs such as mock oranges, *Potentilla*, viburnums, and *Hydrangea paniculata* should do well and also give some shelter to plants below and among them; where the climate is mild and hard frost is uncommon, lavenders, rosemary, and *Cistus* can be added to the list. But in

sites that are regularly buffeted by strong winds, choose plants that are naturally found growing on mountains and hillsides where the wind is incessant: small-leaved cotoneasters, barberries, heathers such as *Calluna* and *Erica*, firethorns, and brooms such as *Genista hispanica* and *Cytisus scoparius*. There are also many alpine rhododendrons.

COASTAL CLIMATES

Perhaps the most problematic gardens are those close to the sea, exposed to salt-laden winds that can damage leaves and bark, killing shrubs. For these gardens, choose shrubs that are highly specialized, many of them from the Mediterranean: lavender,

▲ *ROSMARINUS OFFICINALIS* 'MISS JESSOPP'S UPRIGHT' *Mediterranean plants tolerate dry soil and warm sea winds.*

▶ *HEBE* 'GREAT ORME' *The small, tough-skinned leaves of these evergreens minimize the evaporation caused by drying winds.*

TAMARIX RAMOSISSIMA This summer-flowering tamarisk has small, thin, scale-like leaves, making it highly resistant to salty winds. In nature, wind distorts the growth of its wispy stems, leading to an ungainly shape; they respond well to pruning, however, having adapted well to tolerate the loss of branches broken by storms.

Santolina, tamarisk, and *Phlomis fruticosa*. None of these plants will thrive in cold areas: for these, *Prunus maritima*, *Hydrangea macrophylla*, and *Amelanchier* are useful. Some of the shrub roses, such as *Rosa rugosa*, are also well adapted to conditions in seaside gardens and can be used to supplement other flowering shrubs.

Seaside gardens need shrubs that are naturally resistant to salt winds

Remember that wind, whether mild or strong, is very drying. Water young plants regularly and well. If soil erosion and drying are a problem, use mulches of loose stones. These can also create decorative and naturalistic effects: use coarse gravel between moorland heathers, for example, or coarse sand between seaside shrubs.

SCREENING AND SHELTER

When buying young shrubs for a windy site, choose small, robust, bushy specimens that will stand up well to battering by wind while they establish. Prune back any long, slender stems upon planting. If you need to or want to start off with taller plants, it is worth giving them a short stake for support in the early years, but tie them in loosely so that their stems may build up strength by flexing a little in the wind. You should also erect a temporary screen for them, but choose an open material, such as burlap or plastic strips or mesh between posts, that will break up the wind rather than block it, otherwise the shrubs will grow up overprotected.

Shrubs that are especially good for planting in rows as hedging and screening, protecting other plants in exposed gardens, include *Hippophae rhamnoides*, *Berberis thunbergii*, *Prunus spinosa* and *P. cistena*, *Kerria*, *Elaeagnus commutata*, *Cotinus*, *Spiraea*, and *Hamamelis virginiana*, and in mild areas *Olearia* and *Escallonia*. For more details of wind-resistant shrubs, see *Recommended Flowering Shrubs*, pp.66–69.

LOOKING AFTER SHRUBS

WHICH SHRUB WHERE?

Before you buy any flowering shrub, consider the prevailing conditions of where you want to plant it. Is the position windy or sheltered, in full sun or shade? Is your soil fairly "ordinary" or is it, for example, very dry or acidic (*pp.16–17*)? These factors influence which shrubs you choose because, to put on their best show, they must have growing conditions to meet their needs.

CHOOSING HEALTHY PLANTS

Container-grown shrubs can be bought and planted at almost any time of year, but if you can, choose autumn or spring to plant, when mild weather will not stress the young shrub too much. Shrubs may also be sold with their roots wrapped in plastic with a little soil mix. These can make perfectly good plants, but check that the roots have not dried out, then plant without delay. Buy ideally when plants first appear on the shelves, not after they have been sitting around for some time.

BUYING TIPS

• Look for a shrub with an attractive, well-balanced shape and plenty of new growth. Check that shoot tips are healthy with no sign of scorch or dieback.

• Roots should be well established and healthy but not protrude from the base of the pot.

• The best time to plant shrubs that are fully hardy in your climate is autumn. For more tender shrubs wait until spring, lessening the risk of winter damage.

• Avoid buying shrubs in heavy flower; the flowers will sap the plant's energy while it is getting established and should be removed.

Fresh new growth with healthy shoot tips

Stems are evenly spaced and branch close to ground level

Make sure that shrub has been labeled properly

A GOOD PLANT
This specimen has plentiful, healthy foliage and lots of new growth. The stems are well placed and the pot is a good size for the amount of topgrowth; avoid top-heavy plants.

◀ WELL SHAPED *An attractive form enhances the flowers of* Viburnum plicatum *'Mariesii.'*

PLANTING AND AFTERCARE

ONCE YOU HAVE CHOSEN A SHRUB and the place to plant it, prepare the soil well. This is where the plant is likely to be all its life; good preparation gives it a good start and makes it more able to grow strongly. Container-grown shrubs generally have a pampered existence and when planted, their roots find it hard to penetrate lumpy, uneven, and especially heavy soil; they can stop growing. Do what you can to make their new home conducive to growth.

PLANTING A SHRUB

Improve soil texture around the new shrub's rootball to make it crumbly and moisture-retentive but well-firmed and without air pockets. Make a large hole, and chop up lumps in the soil at the base and around the side; do the same with the soil you use to refill the hole. Mix in one or two shovels of organic matter: well-rotted compost, manure, or mushroom soil. Well-rotted manure is excellent, but not in clods, which often dry out and harden underground. A handful of bonemeal, alfalfa pellets, or chicken manure adds long-lasting nutrients to the soil.

1 **Dig the hole** twice as wide and deep as the plant's pot, and break up the soil at the base and around the sides, working in organic matter. Water the plant in its pot.

2 **To make sure that** the rootball doesn't collapse, place your hand flat across the top of the rootball and ease off the pot then cup your other hand under the rootball.

3 **Adjust the depth** of the hole until the plant sits correctly. Use a stake to make sure that you plant the shrub at the same depth as it was in its container.

4 **Break up the soil** that you dug out of the hole, then shovel it in around the roots. Firm well and evenly all around the plant before watering thoroughly and mulching.

Planting a Shrub in a Container

Planting shrubs in containers means that you can tailor the soil mix to meet needs that your soil cannot: for example, azaleas can be given an acidic soil mix and thus be grown even in an alkaline area. The same acidic soil mix enables blue-flowered hydrangeas to keep their color. For the long term and for the pot's stability, it is better to use a heavier soil-based mix, with a slow-release fertilizer. Don't put a small shrub into a large container, hoping that it will eventually fill it; plants grow more strongly in pots only one or two sizes up from their previous home, large enough to sustain the shrub through at least one year, when it can be potted on. Vigorous shrubs need annual feeding, and all container plants require regular watering and good drainage.

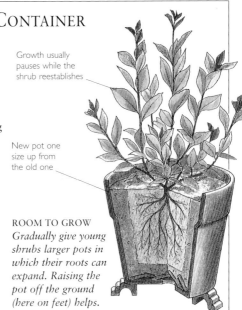

Growth usually pauses while the shrub reestablishes

New pot one size up from the old one

ROOM TO GROW
Gradually give young shrubs larger pots in which their roots can expand. Raising the pot off the ground (here on feet) helps.

Watering and Mulching

All shrubs, even those that are drought-tolerant, need watering during dry spells in their first two or three years. It is better to water deeply once a week than to give frequent small doses. A 2–4in/5–10cm layer of mulch on damp soil round the shrub retains moisture and keeps roots cool: use leafmold, bark chips, or well-rotted manure.

MAKING A BASIN FOR WATER
After planting, make a ridge of soil around the area of the shrub's rootball to hold water while it sinks down to the roots. Do not do this on heavy soils prone to waterlogging.

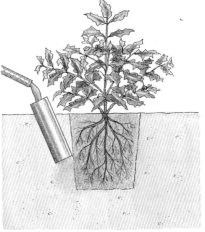

ADDING A WATERING PIPE
Burying a length of drainpipe near the plant and filling it with water from a hose will ensure the water reaches the bottom of the rootball. Water the soil surface as well.

ROUTINE PRUNING

THERE IS LITTLE NEED, usually, to prune healthy young shrubs. However, after one or two growing seasons, there may be unwanted stems to remove. You may need to make only those cuts that keep the plant healthy and well-formed (as on these pages) or choose to prune additionally each year to enhance flowering (see overleaf). Not all shrubs need or enjoy the latter type of pruning: many will flower for years unpruned and naturally groom themselves.

MAKING CORRECT CUTS

Whenever you prune a shrub, whether to remove damaged stems or spent flowers or simply to cut a stem to bring into the house for its flowers or foliage, get into the habit of making well-positioned, clean cuts. If you leave snags they may die back (*see below*), attracting disease. New shoots will grow from the buds you cut to, so look at which way alternate buds face to make the stem grow upward or outward.

OPPOSITE BUDS
Cut straight through the stem just above a pair of buds, leaves, or sideshoots.

ALTERNATE BUDS
Prune just above a bud, leaf, or shoot with a slightly sloping cut, angled toward it.

CUTTING OUT BRANCHES
Don't strain pruners on thick stems: a pair of loppers makes the task much easier.

PRUNING FOR HEALTH

If you cut back stems you see that are dead, damaged, or looking very unhealthy, you may be able to prevent problems from spreading. Cut across cleanly at a suitable point well below the affected part: at the base, or where they spring from a larger branch, or to just above a healthy sideshoot, leaf, or bud.

Tender shoot tip killed by frost

Pruning cut was made too high above buds

▶ FROST DAMAGE
This frost-scorched shoot tip will not recover. Prune it back to just above some completely healthy leaves.

▲ DEAD STUB
Dieback often halts naturally at new shoots: trim off any dead snags.

PRUNING TO SHAPE

Most shrubs, left to their own devices, will develop a natural form that requires little or no attention. In the garden, however, shrubs may outgrow their position or become one-sided from being crowded by other shrubs or shaded by buildings. Some, especially evergreens, may develop leggy branches that spoil their neat shape. Don't be overzealous about pruning out stems unless they get in the way, offend the eye, or look as if wind and weather might break them. Also, never trim a flowering shrub all over in an effort to reduce its size, since you may well be removing the current year's or the next year's flowers. If it's too big, consider a smaller replacement.

◀ OVERLONG SHOOT
Prune back protruding branches deep within the shrub, leaving the fresh cut hidden.

▲ SPRAWLING STEMS
Pruning low down may encourage fresh growth to replace bare, leggy branches.

THINNING AN OVERGROWN SHRUB

The branches of many shrubs, including mock oranges, *Weigela*, forsythia, lilacs, and viburnums, can become too crowded: many of the lower and inner branches become old and woody, and the flowers appear too high up on the shrub. Thinning lets in more air and light, enouraging fresh shoots to flower lower down on the shrub. A really old, neglected shrub is probably best replaced, unless it is one of the few that tolerate drastic pruning (*below*); this will mean the loss of that year's flowers.

THINNING THICKETS
Prune out thick, old branches from the center of the shrub to encourage young stems.

LIGHTENING DENSE GROWTH
Cut back longer, thicker main stems at the junction with healthy-looking sideshoots.

DRASTIC PRUNING

Shrubs that can be cut down in late winter:
Chaenomeles
Cotoneaster
Deutzia
Forsythia
Hydrangea paniculata
Ligustrum
Philadelphus
Potentilla
Ribes sanguineum
Spiraea
Syringa
Viburnum opulus
Vitex

PRUNING FOR FLOWERING

PRUNING CAN ENCOURAGE shrubs to either flower more profusely or to carry larger blooms, but not all shrubs need or tolerate this (*right*) and should only be pruned when necessary (*see previous pages*). Most pruning for better flowers is carried out after flowering. For spring-flowering shrubs, this is best done in early summer, but for late-flowerers delay pruning in cold climates until late winter.

NO PRUNING NECESSARY

These shrubs need no pruning apart from essential cuts made for their health or as noted: *Camellia* need deadheading only to neaten; *Cistus* often resent pruning; *Choisya ternata*; *Daphne* should never be pruned unless absolutely necessary; *Hamamelis*; *Hibiscus syriacus*; *Hydrangea villosa, H. aspera*; *Kolkwitzia amabilis*; *Magnolia; Mahonia* can be pruned hard occasionally to reshape; *Osmanthus;* most *Prunus*; *Skimmia*; *Viburnum carlesii, V. burkwoodii, V. juddii.*

DEADHEADING TO PROLONG FLOWERING

Deadheading is the removal of spent flower-heads before they set seed; if left on, they take nutrition from the plant and inhibit the formation of new flower buds. Deadheading redirects the plant's energies into new growth. This new growth will support the next flush of blooms, either later in the same season or the next year. The prevention of nuisance self-seeding of, for example, buddleias, is a bonus.

PINCHING OUT
Rhododendron and camellia flowers bloom on very short, almost nonexistent stalks. Pinch and twist out the dead flowers very carefully between finger and thumb to avoid damaging other flower and leaf buds below them.

Make clean cuts with pruners

CUTTING BACK FLOWERED STEMS
Buddleias flower well into late summer, albeit in smaller clusters, if you cut off spent blooms just above the next pair of sideshoots.

SHRUBS THAT FLOWER BETTER IF DEADHEADED

For many, deadheading is in addition to the annual pruning of stems (*see following pages*). Always prune cleanly back to healthy sideshoots, leaves, or buds (*see p.30*).
Buddleja davidii
Caryopteris

Ceanothus, only the late-flowering deciduous types such as 'Gloire de Versailles' and 'Marie Simon'
Choisya ternata
Clethra alnifolia
Hydrangea macrophylla,
  H. paniculata

Kalmia
Lavandula (lavender) trim the whole plant with shears
Lespedeza thunbergii
Rhododendron
Spiraea, only the late-flowering types
Syringa (lilac)

Pruning Shrubs that Flower on Old Wood

Shrubs that flower in the spring or early summer develop their embryonic flower buds on stems that have grown and matured during the previous summer, so if you cut back these stems in winter or early spring, you will be removing potential flowering stems. All green-leaved evergreens flower in this way, but so do many deciduous shrubs; forsythia is a classic example (*see right and below*). Prune these shrubs immediately after flowering, in the spring or early summer. Pruning should not be done later than early summer; otherwise, the new growth that pruning encourages will not have enough time to grow and mature to bloom the next year.

Immediately after flowering the new growth will have already started. Prune long, old flowered shoots back to a vigorous-looking sideshoot.

Spent flowers on previous year's shoots

New shoots

LAST YEAR'S LEGACY
Forsythia is a typical example of a plant that flowers on old wood, well before the new season's shoots start to grow.

PRUNE AFTER FLOWERING

Deciduous shrubs that flower on last year's wood and can be pruned as below include:
Chaenomeles, grown as freestanding shrubs.
Deutzia all types, treat as *Philadelphus*.
Forsythia, can be pruned hard or trimmed, or a mixture of both, as in the diagram below.
Kolkwitzia
Philadelphus, prune out main branches at the base every year.
Spiraea, the spring-flowering types.
Syringa, prune if overgrown, or just deadhead.

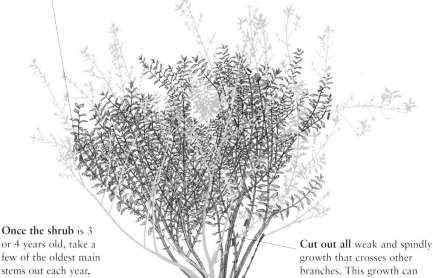

Once the shrub is 3 or 4 years old, take a few of the oldest main stems out each year, pruning right to the base of the shrub.

Cut out all weak and spindly growth that crosses other branches. This growth can often die inside the shrub for lack of light.

PRUNING SHRUBS THAT FLOWER ON NEW WOOD

On many shrubs, new shoots grow from the old wood and flower all in one season. You can prune after flowering, but in colder climates it is best to wait until the worst of winter is over. With some, you may prune lightly or, for fewer but larger flowers, prune hard. Others, especially some small gray-leaved shrubs (*see facing page*), should be treated almost like herbaceous perennials and pruned close to the ground.

FLOWERING ON NEW WOOD

Buddleja davidii Prune down to a main stump (*see facing page*).
Ceanothus, deciduous kinds Can be pruned hard to encourage fewer but more vigorous flowering stems.
Mophead hydrangeas (*H. macrophylla*) Prune back to about half the previous height (*below*), varying heights of different stems.
Hydrangea paniculata Can be pruned hard like buddleia, or down to new, healthy buds as they break, like the mopheads.
Hypericum can be pruned hard or lightly.

Prune the following back to 6in/15cm from the ground:
Fuchsias, the so-called hardy types such as
   F. magellanica
Indigofera heterantha
Lespedeza thunbergii
Perovskia atriplicifolia
Spiraea, the late summer-flowering types

NEW GROWTH
Shrubs that flower on new growth can usually be identified by the fact that they bloom from midsummer onward, at the tips of fresh young shoots – such as this Buddleja × weyeriana.

PRUNING *HYDRANGEA MACROPHYLLA*
The stems of mophead hydrangeas should be cut back to the first really healthy pair of fat, rounded buds, which are obvious in late winter or early spring. Remove any weak, unhealthy shoots completely.

Using sharp pruners, prune to just above a pair of large, rounded buds, removing the old dried flowerheads.

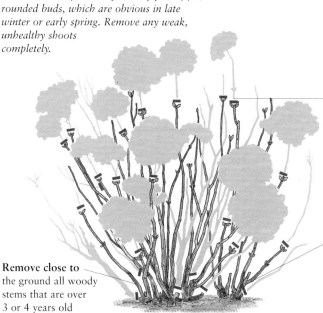

Prune out all thin, spindly wood and dead twigs.

Remove close to the ground all woody stems that are over 3 or 4 years old

PRUNING *BUDDLEJA DAVIDII*
*Butterfly bushes are very vigorous and can produce new shoots
6½ft/2m tall and more in a single season, even when pruned to within
12in/30cm of the ground. You don't need to prune them, but it does
give you a more manageable shrub with big, fat flower spikes.*

Prune back all stems
that grew the
previous year to
healthy breaking buds
if you can see them.

Cut out very old
woody stumps from
previous years with
loppers or a saw.

SMALL GRAY-LEAVED SHRUBS

Many smaller gray-leaved shrubs derive
from coastal plants that are accustomed to
being cut down naturally by salt winds, so
they usually flower, for safety, on new
stems. However, not all respond well to
being cut back hard into bare wood.
Regular trimming will keep them in good
shape, usually for several years, but as they
get old and leggy, they should
be replaced.

PRUNE LIGHTLY
*Trim lavender
lightly after
flowering and
again in early
spring, but leave
plenty of leafy
growth: hard
pruning is risky.*

PRUNE HARD
Santolina *can be pruned
hard to within
2in/5cm of
the ground in
spring and
trimmed
throughout
the summer.*

Plants that should be trimmed:
*Calluna • Cytisus • Erica • Genista •
Helichrysum splendidum • Lavandula •
Leptospermum • Olearia • Potentilla •
Rosmarinus*

Plants that can be cut back hard:
Brachyglottis 'Sunshine' • *Caryopteris •
Ceratostigma • Elaeagnus angustifolia •
Perovskia • Phlomis fruticosa • Santolina*
(not *S. incana*) • *Teucrium fruticans*

WALL-TRAINING SHRUBS

TRAINING A SHRUB closely against a wall or fence, so that it grows flat, involves some regular pruning; only some shrubs will tolerate this and still flower well. Fan- or espalier-training is particularly useful where there is only a narrow area of ground. Remember that the soil by a wall may be dry and full of construction material, so improve the soil well with organic matter (*see p.28*) before planting.

FOR WALL-TRAINING

Chaenomeles speciosa
Ceanothus, most upright evergreen types
Cotoneaster, the small-leaved kinds
Forsythia suspensa
Jasminum nudiflorum
Garrya elliptica
Itea ilicifolia
Magnolia grandiflora, a slow-growing tree
Pyracantha, most
See Recommended Flowering Shrubs *pp.60–63.*

TRAINING IN A NEW YOUNG SHRUB

Have supports such as a trellis or wires, strong enough to support the mature shrub, in place before planting. Choose a plant that seems naturally to grow in one plane; choose its "best" side to face outward, and cut off any shoots that stick out behind. Plant the shrub (*see p.28*) 12–18in/30–45cm from the wall. Spread all sideways-growing branches out evenly, gently pulling them down as far toward the horizontal as they will safely go, then tie in. Do not push or tuck shoots behind struts or wires; they may be damaged and, as they thicken, they will push the support away from the wall and be difficult to prune out. Prune away any superfluous or forward-facing shoots.

Tie in the stems (here of a *Ceanothus*), not too tight, with garden twine in figure-eight knots.

Remove any shoots that stick out in front.

Prune the tips of the tied-in stems to encourage denser growth.

Cut off shoots at the base of the shrub.

PRUNING AN ESTABLISHED WALL-TRAINED SHRUB

Taking care to prune at the right time of year for each shrub, encourage the shrub to stay flat to the wall and not too sparse in the middle. Remove any growth that crosses over other shoots, and cut the tips off of lateral and vertical shoots. Some shrubs, such as *Chaenomeles*, are easy to train and can be pruned quite hard once a year. Too much pruning can damage plants such as *Ceanothus* and hinder flowering, and in others it induces too much leafy growth. Pruning lightly in late winter and summer will tame this.

Spur-pruned stem

Unpruned stem

SPUR-PRUNING
Some shrubs that flower on old wood, such as Chaenomeles *and* Pyracantha, *respond well if, in summer, you shorten their leafy new shoots; they flower better, and flowers and fruits are shown off well. This makes them ideal for wall-training.*

Prune sideshoots back to two or three leaves or buds, depending on the time of year.

Cut out forward- facing shoots that cannot be trained sideways and tied in without crowding.

Tie in stems as they grow

Trim shoots where they grow beyond the shrub's allotted space

RECOMMENDED FLOWERING SHRUBS

CHOOSING PLANTS

THE RANGE OF SHRUBS here has been divided into various categories, but there is plenty of overlap. For example, many of the *Evergreen Favorites* will tolerate some shade, while *Shrubs for Shade* includes only those plants that actually prefer less light. Average heights for the most popular types of each shrub have been given, but check labels before you buy to make sure you have not picked a dwarf or especially vigorous kind.

THE CATEGORIES

- **Deciduous** and **Evergreen Favorites** contain reliable garden classics.
- **Fragrant Shrubs** includes the best for scent.
- **Shrubs for Shade** and for **Acidic Soil** contain problem-solving shrubs for special conditions.
- **Shrubs for Walls** may be formally fan- or espalier-trained or loosely tied in; some need a sheltered position.
- **Shrubs for Windy Gardens** that need mild coastal conditions are also good for **Dry Sites**; others will stand up to cold winds.
- **Shrubs for Containers** contains small or particularly suitable types of the shrubs mentioned in previous categories.

SUITING THE SITE
Use this selection of recommended shrubs to match plants to the conditions in your garden and the site you have in mind, or to see whether a favorite plant can be given a suitable home somewhere in your yard. Shrubs are great low-maintenance plants for the backs of borders and near walls and fences, where other plants might be difficult to tend. This Ceanothus *'Puget Blue' also benefits from the shelter of the brick wall.*

◀ PLANNING THE YEAR Caryopteris *'Arthur Simmonds' flowers from summer into autumn.*

DECIDUOUS FAVORITES

BUDDLEJA   Z6–9

Most buddleias grow about 10ft/3m tall, with an arching habit, although **B. davidii** var. **nanhoensis** is dwarf. They like full sun and well-drained soil but are otherwise unfussy. **B. davidii** is the most popular, with spikes of fragrant blooms on new wood (*see* '**Fascinating**', *p.6*). Prune them hard in early spring (*see p.35*). Flowers are mauve, white, pink, blue, or reddish purple; '**White Profusion**' (*see p.22*), '**Empire Blue**', and '**Pink Delight**' are recommended.

Another option is **Buddleja alternifolia** (*below*), spring-flowering, with small grayish leaves and bunches of tiny lilac-purple flowers all along long arching stems that grew the previous year, so this species must be pruned as for shrubs that flower on old, not new, wood (*see p.33*).

CHAENOMELES   Z5–9

Easily grown on all except wet soils as free-standing shrubs about 8ft/2.5m tall, *Chaenomeles* (also called flowering quince or japonica) are also often wall-trained; *C. speciosa* types are best for this (*see p.60*). Clustered, appleblossom-like flowers on short, stubby twigs all along the branches open in late winter and early spring in red, pinks or, in '**Nivalis**', snow white. For a small form, look for '**Geisha Girl**', with sugar-pink flowers. *C.* × *superba* '**Crimson and Gold**' (*below*) is one of the most striking, with cupped flowers of a very bright scarlet and a more bushy, thicketlike habit. *Chaenomeles* flower on old wood and can be pruned, hard if necessary, to shape or to thin after flowering (*see p.31*). In summer, shortening new leafy shoots (*see p.37*) encourages more flowers.

DEUTZIA   Z5–8

These are tough, easy-to-grow shrubs, typically around 5ft/1.5m tall, for sun or partial shade and any fertile soil. In shade they still flower well and develop an attractive, open habit. Prune some old stems to the base of the shrub after flowering (*see p.33*). *D.* × *elegantissima* '**Rosealind**' (*below*) is compact, with erect sprays of rose-pink flowers in early summer. There are many others, flowering in either pink or white. Choose **D. gracilis** for white flowers. Other good pink-flowered *Deutzia* are '**Mont Rose**', with warm-toned flowers freely borne on a graceful bush, and *D.* × *rosea* '**Carminea**', with pale rose-pink flowers. Both have purplish buds. *D.* × *magnifica* is a taller shrub, with double pink flowers set densely along the branches.

BUDDLEJA ALTERNIFOLIA

CHAENOMELES × *SUPERBA* '*CRIMSON AND GOLD*'

DEUTZIA × *ELEGANTISSIMA* '*ROSEALIND*'

FORSYTHIA   Z5–9

Forsythias are rather awkwardly shaped shrubs of varying sizes but are much valued for their cheery yellow, weather-resistant flowers all along the bare twigs in late winter and early spring. If they are pruned regularly after flowering (see p.33), the flowers, on sideshoots from old wood, can smother the entire bush. They may also be left unpruned. Forsythias thrive in most soils in sun or shade. In shade they develop a more open, elegant habit with sparser flowering, which some find more attractive. There are many hybrid forsythias bred for bigger, brighter flowers, such as the *F.* × *intermedia* types: 'Lynwood', with a very dense habit, 'Arnold Giant' (see p.7), and 'Arnold Dwarf'. *F. suspensa* (below) has much paler yellow flowers and a rather lax, pendulous habit. Over 6½ft/2m high and wide, it can be tied against a wall to prevent sprawling.

FUCHSIA   Z7–9

The so-called "hardy" fuchsias are beautiful garden plants but need protection where marginally hardy with a blanket of dry straw, compost, or soil over winter. They also make good container shrubs (see p.75), which can be moved under cover. In mild areas, *F. magellanica* (below) may retain its woody framework over winter, but it is more usually cut down by cold: not a problem, since the shrub can be pruned low and will reshoot from ground level, growing to 5ft/1.5m tall. It mixes well with herbaceous plantings, doing best in full sun though tolerating light or part-day shade. Among the best are the varieties *versicolor*, with white and silvery pink leaf markings that contrast beautifully with the red and purple of the flowers, and *molinae*, with pink flowers; 'Genii', with golden leaves; and white-flowered 'Hawkshead'.

HIBISCUS   Z5–9

Erect shrubs, growing quite slowly up to 10ft/3m tall, bearing large, bowl- to trumpet-shaped flowers in summer and into autumn. The leaves are deeply lobed and dark green. *H. syriacus* must have abundant sunshine to flower best, so it should be planted in full sun. *H. rosa-sinensis* cultivars are hardy to 50°F/10°C. Both make good container plants (see p.75).

H. syriacus types respond well to pruning to shape in early spring before the buds break. They thrive best in most well-drained soils. 'Diana' (below) is one of the largest-flowered hybrids. 'Jeanne d'Arc' is a semi-double white. 'Blue Bird' (see p.6), also called 'Oiseau Bleu', is a clear lavender-blue, while 'Woodbridge' has darker crimson flowers. Many of them, such as 'Blue Bird' and the white 'Red Heart' have maroon veins and blotches at the petal bases.

FORSYTHIA SUSPENSA

FUCHSIA MAGELLANICA

HIBISCUS SYRIACUS 'DIANA'

HYDRANGEA   Z below

Hydrangeas are versatile shrubs, growing in almost any soil or position. Some in particular are excellent for shade (*see p.64*). The most popular types for borders or containers (*see p.76*) are the macrophyllas (Z6–9): rounded, up to 6½ft/2m tall, with lacecap or mophead flowers, in white (try '**Lanarth White**' or '**Madame Emile Mouillère**', with a pink eye), pink ('**King George**' is good), or, on acidic soil only, blue (look for '**Blue Wave**' and '**Nikko Blue**'.) Prune them in late winter (*see p.34*). *H. paniculata* (Z4–8) is another fine shrub for general garden use; very tough, up to 10ft/3m tall, or prune it hard in late winter to keep at only 6½ft/2m. Flowering on new wood, it produces dense cones of white florets, especially large and striking in '**Grandiflora**', and in '**Pink Diamond**' (*below*) quickly turning pink as they fade. The dried, brown flowerheads are decorative in winter.

INDIGOFERA   Z6–9

Although not startling plants, *Indigofera* are elegant, useful in dry gardens, and flower when few other shrubs do. In winter, they can be cut down by cold but spring up again from the base, flowering on the current season's growth. Thus they can pruned hard in late winter or, in warmer regions, left unpruned to form taller, open shrubs. *I. heterantha* grows up to 10ft/3m tall. It may carry its mauve-pink flowers well into late summer. *I. decora* (*below*) is slender and open-growing, for a sunny site and any well-drained soil, doing especially well on dry ground. It has arching shoots up to 6½ft/2m tall, with pretty, lush leaflets and sprays of small, pink-purple pealike flowers in midsummer. *Indigofera* blend well with grasses or hardy fuchsias. The flowers look lovely set against dark purple foliage; try growing them with *Cotinus coggygria* 'Royal Purple'.

KERRIA   Z4–9

An old cottage garden favorite, *Kerria japonica* is a charming, twiggy dense bush, about 6½ft/2m tall, with golden yellow flowers in spring. The stems are upright, wiry, and bright green, and the leaves are fresh and pointed. Although deciduous, its green twigs look good in winter. Tolerant of most soil types, including very alkaline soil, it flowers well in some shade. There are cultivars with silver- and golden-variegated leaves. The former, '**Picta**', is a small bush, a little more vulnerable to cold in winter. '**Golden Guinea**' (*below*) has very large flowers. The double-flowered cultivar, '**Pleniflora**', actually arrived in the West from China before the species. It is a much more vigorous shrub with a habit of suckering all around the main plant: this can become a nuisance. The double flowers do, however, last longer.

HYDRANGEA PANICULATA 'PINK DIAMOND'

INDIGOFERA DECORA

KERRIA JAPONICA 'GOLDEN GUINEA'

KOLKWITZIA   Z5–9

Sometimes known as the beautybush, **Kolkwitzia amabilis** is a rounded shrub, growing up to 8ft/2.5m tall and wide, with dense twiggy growth that bears clusters of small, pale purplish pink flowers with yellow throats in late spring. **'Pink Cloud'** (*below*) has more delicate coloring and is more reliable in its flowering. This and **'Rosea'** are the ones to look for.

   Kolkwitzia grow in any soil, including very alkaline soil. They may take a few years to settle down and flower well. Spring-flowering shrubs, they should be pruned every year once established to remove some of the oldest wood immediately after flowering. Similar in some ways to *Deutzia* and *Weigela*, *Kolkwitzia* are often grown with these or with shrub roses and lilacs, which all enjoy similar growing conditions, making a fine spring display.

KOLKWITZIA AMABILIS
'PINK CLOUD'

POTENTILLA   Z3–7

Potentilla fruticosa is a small but invaluable, dense, rounded shrub, about 3ft/1m tall, carrying small, roselike flowers through summer. It will grow in any soil, and although happiest in full sun will thrive in partial shade. It can tend to look a little ragged in winter so is best given a trim then, or in early spring. Use shears, removing all the old seedpods and generally neatening it up: this will make it more bushy and improve flowering.

   The species has pale yellow flowers, but there are other yellows, pinks, reddish oranges, and white available, most between 2ft/60cm and 4ft/1.2m tall. Recommended are **'Elizabeth'**, canary yellow, **'Daydawn'**, a light peach, and **'Primrose Beauty'** (*see p.77*). The hybrid **'Abbotswood'** has gray-green leaves and pure white flowers. **'Tangerine'** (*below*) is a soft orange; its color is best in some shade.

POTENTILLA FRUTICOSA
'TANGERINE'

PRUNUS   Z below

There are several lovely evergreen shrubby *Prunus* (*see p.50*), but the deciduous types more closely resemble plum and cherry trees. **Prunus × cistena** (Z4–8) (*below*) grows up to 5ft/1.5m tall, with dark purple foliage that contrasts with the small, pink-white flowers that open with the leaves in early spring. It grows almost anywhere but prefers full sun in an open position. It will withstand salty winds, as does the similar beach plum, **P. maritima** (Z3–6). It can be pruned hard, removing old wood after flowering. *P. mume* (Z6–8) flowers even earlier, with fragrant pink-purple flowers all over bare stems, from new wood down to wood that is 3 or even 4 years old. *P. tenella* **'Fire Hill'** (Z6–8) is more thicketlike, carrying wands of rich pink flowers. *P. triloba* **'Multiplex'** (Z6–8) is a double-flowered, clear pink dwarf cherry, often available grafted onto a short trunk.

PRUNUS × CISTENA

RIBES
Z below

The flowering currants are upright shrubs, mostly about 6½ft/2m tall, although **R. alpinum** (Z2–6), with greenish yellow flowers, is much smaller, to 3ft/90cm. **R. sanguineum** (Z6–8) is a popular early spring-flowering shrub, despite its "catty" scent, with deep rose-pink flowers in small clusters that dangle at first, and later stand up off the upright growth. It is a very easy shrub to grow in almost all well-drained soils in sun or partial shade. There are pretty white- and pale pink-flowered varieties; for deep, rich color try **'King Edward VII'**, lower-growing with crimson flowers, and **'Pulborough Scarlet'**, deep red. **'Brocklebankii'** (*below*) is golden-leaved; its foliage tends to burn in full sun. Much more sweetly scented is **R. odoratum** (Z5–8), an erect shrub with tiny yellow flowers. **R. speciosum** (Z6–9) has rich red, fuchsialike flowers in clusters in early spring; it likes a sheltered spot.

RUBUS
Z below

The flowers of *Rubus* grown ornamentally are very similar to those of their relatives, the brambles, but in some cases the stems are thornless. Although their stems are long and flexible, they make largely self-supporting plants rather than scrambling through others. **R. 'Benenden'** (Z5–9) (*below*) is a large shrub, up to 10ft/3m high and 13ft/4m wide, that carries pure white flowers with a central boss of golden yellow stamens in mid- to late spring. The flowers are produced singly on strong, arching stems, with leaves that are three- to five-lobed. Grow it in any fertile soil in full sun or partial shade. Spring-flowering, it should be pruned immediately after flowering. For a similar shrub with pink flowers, look for **'Walberton Red'**. **R. thibetanus** (Z7–9) is more erect, with white flowers, beautiful gray leaves, and prickly stems with a white coating.

SPIRAEA
Z4–8

Spiraea japonica is a very robust summer-flowering shrub, tolerating most soil types and enjoying sun or partial shade. It grows to up to 5½ft/1.75m tall; many of its cultivars only grow to 3ft/1m at most but have the bonus of beautiful, bright foliage. The pink flowers (white in **var. albiflora**) form in clusters, set against leaves that in **'Goldflame'** (*below*) are rich yellow-orange fading to orange-green, or in **'Anthony Waterer'** are bronze when young, then green sometimes edged in cream. These can be pruned hard in winter to encourage intense leaf color and keep them compact, and the flowers will still form. Others are spring-flowering, so prune out old wood after flowering. Usually white-flowered, they include **S. 'Arguta'**, small with slender arching branches smothered in tiny white flowers, and **S. × vanhouttei**, similar but a larger, sturdier plant.

RIBES SANGUINEUM 'BROCKLEBANKII'

RUBUS 'BENENDEN'

SPIRAEA JAPONICA 'GOLDFLAME'

VIBURNUM · Z below

Every garden should include at least one viburnum. Many of the deciduous types have good autumn leaf color; some, such as *V. opulus* (Z4–8), have bright fruits. They grow in most soils. Height and habit vary, but flowers are similar in all: small florets in rounded or lacy, flat-topped clusters in spring. They are pure white or flushed pink. After flowering, old wood can be pruned back if necessary. *V. macrocephalum* (Z7–9) is rounded, to 10ft/ 3m tall. In warmer areas it may be semi-evergreen; in colder areas it needs shelter and sun. *V. × carlcephalum* (Z6–8) is similar but more shade-tolerant. For a tiered shape, grow *V. plicatum* (Z5–8), especially 'Lanarth', 'Mariesii' (*see p.27*), 'Pink Beauty' (*below*), and 'Summer Snowflake', which flowers later than the others, all to 10ft/3m tall, developing graceful, horizontal branches with white or pinkish white flowers.

WEIGELA · Z4–9

These are easy, decorative shrubs growing up to 6½ft/2m tall and wide, for most soils in either sun or partial shade. They flower in early summer on the previous year's growth, so they should be pruned after flowering (*see p.33*), removing a few old stems to encourage new growth from the base of the shrub. Once mature, they are best pruned every year. For good flower color, look for 'Eva Rathke' (*below*), slow-growing and and compact; 'Abel Carrière', with dark pink flowers that gradually fade; and 'Bristol Ruby', with rich crimson flowers. The best white is 'Mont Blanc'. Other cultivars have distinctive foliage, the most popular and harmonious being 'Florida Variegata', with pink flowers and cream-edged leaves; it needs partial shade. Low-growing *W. florida* 'Foliis Purpureis' has purple leaves.

MORE CHOICES

Berberis (see p.66)
Cotoneaster (see p.60)
Genista (see p.67)
Lavatera (see p.71)
Philadelphus (see p.54)
Syringa (see p.55)

Ceanothus (Z7–10)

Deciduous *Ceanothus* grow well in any well-drained soil, given full sun. They bear flowers in late summer that are similar to those of the evergreens (*see p.60*), but their leaves are larger and often color well in autumn, and their habit is much more upright and open-branched. They are excellent for mixing in the flower border. They grow up to 10ft/3m tall, or can be pruned hard in early spring for a smaller bush with fewer, showier flowers. Look for 'Gloire de Versailles' (blue-flowered) and 'Marie Simon' (pink).

Cotinus (Z5–8)

Smoke bushes grow to about 10ft/3m tall, although the purple-leaved types (*see p.14*) are often pruned hard in spring for a smaller bush with bigger and brighter leaves. Growing well in sun or light shade, they are covered by a haze of tiny pink flowers in summer. The foliage of the green-leaved types colors beautifully in autumn.

Nandina domestica (Z6–9)

Heavenly bamboo is a clump-forming shrub up to 6½ft/2m tall for sun or shade, thriving especially in areas with acidic soil conditions and hot summers. It produces sprays of white flowers in spring, followed by bright berries, and has airy, divided leaves that are orange-red when young and in autumn.

VIBURNUM PLICATUM 'PINK BEAUTY'

WEIGELA 'EVA RATHKE'

EVERGREEN FAVORITES

BERBERIS   Z7–9

Evergreen barberries are valuable, thorny shrubs. **B. darwinii** (*below*) is perhaps the most beautiful, growing up to 6½ft/2m tall, with small, shiny, three-pointed leaves, and brilliant orange flowers in spring. In autumn, these are followed by blue-black berries. Barberries are easy to grow, thriving in full sun or shade in any well-drained soil. Some can get leggy, so it is important to prune them after flowering to encourage a more rounded, dense habit. **B. × stenophylla** (*see p.8*) makes an intruder-proof hedge; it has many forms, mostly with orange-yellow flowers. Among the best are 'Irwinii', with a more compact habit, and 'Etna', graceful and free-flowering. For a confined space, **B. buxifolia** 'Pygmaea' is small, no more than 3ft (1m) tall and wide, with yellow flowers.

CALLISTEMON   Z9–11

Callistemon, all native to Australia, are very distinctive shrubs known as bottlebrushes, with narrow, pointed, evergreen leaves and cylindrical fluffy spikes of flowers throughout summer. Most, such as the popular **C. rigidus** (*see p.20*), have red flowers. **C. pallidus** and **C. salignus** have creamy yellow flowers. **C. citrinus** 'Splendens' (*below*) has leaves that are lemon-scented when crushed. The hard, gray, nut-like seedheads remain around the lower stems for years, new flowers being produced above them. *Callistemon* are happy in most soils except alkaline ones. They prefer full sun and are remarkably drought-resistant. They can be pruned in early spring. *Callistemon* are most often seen as freestanding shrubs but, because of their flexible stems, lend themselves to fan-training, tied in to a trellis.

CAMELLIA   Z7–8

Camellias are lovely shrubs, many up to 16ft/5m tall, with glossy leaves and cup-shaped flowers in many colors in spring. The opening flower buds are prone to frost damage, but there is often a succession of buds to follow. They prefer acidic to neutral soil, especially with plenty of organic matter such as leafmold, in open woodland. If grown in full sun, keep the roots moist and cool with an organic mulch. If your soil is limy, grow camellias in pots or barrels (*see p.75*), where they look very handsome, not just in flower, but because their foliage and form is so fine. They make elegant conservatory plants. There are hundreds of varieties of **C. japonica**, flowering mostly in pink, white, or red. **C. × williamsii** hybrids have a longer flowering season and are ideal for shade (*see p.64*).

BERBERIS DARWINII

CALLISTEMON CITRINUS 'SPLENDENS'

CAMELLIA JAPONICA 'ADOLPHE AUDUSSON'

CHOISYA   Z9–10

Known as
Mexican orange
blossom, these
are rounded
shrubs with
shiny three-lobed leaves,
aromatic when crushed. The
small white flowers, carried in
bunches through late spring
into early summer, are sweetly
fragrant. '**Aztec Pearl**' (*below*)
has narrower leaves on a
slightly smaller plant than
Choisya ternata, which is a
luxuriant evergreen growing
up to 6½ft/2m tall, very
suitable for city gardens
where it may receive extra
warmth and shelter. In more
open and colder areas it is
prone to cold damage. It will
grow on most soils and, once
established, is fairly tolerant
of dry conditions. There is
no need to prune unless it
becomes too large or ungainly,
especially in shade. Pruning
stems back to new sideshoots
encourages a neater habit.
'**Sundance**' has golden new
growth; it is more compact
and slower growing, excellent
for containers (*see p.75*).

COTONEASTER   Z below

*Cotoneaster
conspicuus*
(Z6–8)
(*below*) is
perhaps the
most beautiful of the small-
leaved, evergreen cotoneasters:
a wide-spreading shrub to 5ft/
1.5m tall, with arching
growth covered in tiny white
flowers in early summer; these
are much more conspicuous
than on many other
cotoneasters, for example,
C. horizontalis (Z5–7) (*see
Shrubs for Wall-training,
p.60*). They are followed by
persistent red berries in
autumn. Cotoneasters are
happy on virtually all soils. In
mass plantings, they make a
good groundcover. Prune, if
necessary, just after flowering
in spring. *C. linearifolius*
(Z6–8) has tiny leaves but
large fruits; wider than it is
tall, it is good for covering
banks or draping over walls.
C. salicifolius (Z6–8) and
'**Exburyensis**' (*see p.12*) are
much taller (to 16ft/5m)
and more graceful, with
large leaves.

ELAEAGNUS   Z7–10

Evergreen
Elaeagnus are
fast-growing
and suitable
for most soils
in sun or shade. Up to 13ft/
4m tall, they form bold
backgrounds for other plants.
They do not need pruning,
but they can be trimmed to
shape and will tolerate the
cutting of stems for flower
arrangements. *Elaeagnus* ×
ebbingei is more often
thought of as a foliage plant
since its small, yellowish
cream flowers are hidden
among the leaves in autumn.
However, the insignificant
appearance of the flowers is
made up for by their intensely
sweet fragrance. Other
evergreen *Elaeagnus* also have
attractive foliage. *E.* ×
ebbingei '**Limelight**' (*below*)
has greenish yellow splashes
in the center of its leaves.
E. pungens '**Maculata**' is
especially vigorous, with
leaves splashed with yellow
in the center; '**Variegata**'
and '**Dicksonii**' have leaves
edged in yellow.

CHOISYA '*AZTEC PEARL*'

COTONEASTER CONSPICUUS

ELAEAGNUS × *EBBINGEI*
'*LIMELIGHT*'

ESCALLONIA — Z8–9

'Apple Blossom'
(*below*) is one
of the prettiest
members of
the genus,
shrubs mostly 6½–10ft/2–3m
high with an open arching
habit, carrying small flowers
along their stems. The leaves
are glossy and are aromatic in
warm weather. For dark pink,
almost red flowers look for
E. rubra **'Crimson Spire'**
(with more upright growth,
also suitable for hedging); for
white flowers, plant *E.* **'Iveyi'**.
All of these plants are
excellent for seaside gardens
in mild areas; they are highly
resistant to salt spray. Inland
and in colder areas they need
winter protection, or grow
against a sunny wall. They
prefer full sun in most soils,
and once established are quite
drought tolerant. Some are a
little ungainly but can be
pruned to improve their shape
(*see p.33*). The flowers are
borne mostly on the current
season's growth, so old stems
can be cut out after flowering
or in very early spring.

GARRYA — Z8–10

An evergreen
with handsome,
leathery leaves,
Garrya elliptica
(*below*) bears a
profusion of flowers in the
form of long catkins in late
winter. The male and female
flowers are carried on
different plants, those on
male forms being more
conspicuous. The best of
these is **'James Roof'**. Where
marginally hardy, they benefit
from the extra protection
provided by a warm wall.
They are not fussy as to soil
type, as long it is well-drained
and reasonably fertile.
Tolerant of atmospheric
pollution and some exposure
to salt winds, they also grow
in some shade, flowering well,
for instance, on a wall that
receives only morning sun.
Prune, if necessary, in early
spring after flowering, but not
too hard; rather than training
them formally against a wall,
tie them in loosely. Growing
to 10–16m/3–5m, they make
good hedges, provided that
you do not prune too formally.

GREVILLEA — Z below

One of the hardier
grevilleas, *G.*
rosmarinifolia
(Z9–10),
(*below*) is a
beautiful shrub for mild
regions, thriving where
marginally hardy in a
sheltered spot such as near a
wall, with more elaborate
protection in more open
areas, or in a conservatory. It
has narrow, needlelike gray-
green leaves, complemented
for many weeks in late spring
and summer by spikes of
cream to light crimson
flowers, shaped a little like
those of a honeysuckle. For
richer red flower color, look
for **'Canberra Gem'** (Z9–11).
All of them prefer a sunny site
in well-drained soil that is not
too limy. Growing up to 6½ft/
2m, and more in mild areas,
they associate well with other
plants liking dry conditions,
such as *Callistemon*, rosemary,
and *Cistus*. Pruning is generally
unnecessary. Their leaves may
be spine-tipped and can cause
skin irritation, so site carefully
and wear gloves to handle.

ESCALLONIA
'APPLE BLOSSOM'

GARRYA ELLIPTICA

GREVILLEA ROSMARINIFOLIA

HYPERICUM Z below

Most of these thrive in almost any soil, in full sun or partial shade and, since they flower on new wood in summer, can be pruned hard in late winter or after flowering in autumn. Almost all have yellow flowers; *H. × inodorum* 'Elstead' (Z7–9) also bears brilliant salmon-red fruits at the tips of the shoots. 'Hidcote' (Z6–9) (*below*) is a superb plant, deservedly one of the most popular of flowering shrubs. Up to 6½ft/2m wide and tall, it is semi-evergreen, more prone to losing its leaves in colder areas. It bears golden yellow saucer-shaped flowers throughout summer and into autumn. *H. calycinum* (Z5–9) is a dwarf, creeping shrub with similar flowers ideal as a groundcover, although it can become a spreading nuisance. *H. × moserianum* 'Tricolor' (Z7–9) is also low-growing but much less vigorous, up to about 30in/75cm tall, with leaves edged in pink and cream.

ITEA Z below

Itea ilicifolia (Z7–9) (*below*) is a beautiful shrub, to 10ft/3m or more in height, with rather lax stems and leaves that are hollylike with small prickles. Its narrow, hanging flower clusters, borne in late summer, look rather like catkins, up to 12in/30cm long and made up of tiny greenish cream flowers that have a light honeylike fragrance. It grows well in full sun or partial shade but, like many Chinese plants, prefers conditions that are not too dry or too hot. Prune after flowering in autumn or early spring, but only to maintain the shape of the plant and to remove very old growth once the shrub matures. A North American species, *I. virginica* (Z6–9) must be grown in acidic soil; its flowers are more erect and conspicuous than those of *I. ilicifolia*. *I. virginica* 'Henry's Garnet' has larger flowers and excellent red-purple autumn color.

MAHONIA Z below

Handsome foliage shrubs year-round, these come into their own in cooler weather, with spires of whorled flower clusters, clear yellow and smelling of honey and lily-of-the-valley. During winter the glossy, spiny leaves also often have a rich reddish tone, especially in open sites. *M. aquifolium* (Z6–9) (*below*) is one of the hardiest, but while it is often used as underplanting for woodland where it must thrive on neglect, it enjoys being looked after. Improving the soil and using a general fertilizer encourages good foliage and flowers. Up to 6½ft/2m tall, like most of the genus it needs frequent pruning to maintain a good shape. It can be planted in sun or shade in any soil as long as it is not too wet. *M. japonica* (Z7–8) and the hybrids *M. × media* 'Charity' (*see p.13*) and 'Underway' (*see p.23*), (both Z8–9), enjoy similar conditions.

HYPERICUM 'HIDCOTE'

ITEA ILICIFOLIA

MAHONIA AQUIFOLIUM

OSMANTHUS   Z7–9

Osmanthus delavayi (*below*) is a dense, bushy

evergreen, up to 6½ft/2m tall and 10ft/3m wide, with small leaves and clusters of small, tubular flowers in spring, which are highly fragrant – altogether, a lovely shrub for almost any soil, including alkaline, as long as it is not too dry. The flowers are borne more freely in an open, sunny position, but it is quite happy in partial shade. It is extremely slow to establish in its first few years, so do not prune young plants unless absolutely necessary. Once mature it can be (though does not need to be) pruned after flowering to give it a more compact shape. Similar but larger is *O.* × *burkwoodii*, though it is not as delicate and sweetly scented as *O. delavayi*. *O. heterophyllus* has the same type of flowers but more hollylike leaves, splashed with cream in '**Variegatus**'.

OZOTHAMNUS   Z below

Ozothamnus ledifolius (**Z9–10**) (*below*) forms a dense bush up to

5ft/1.5m tall, with small, succulent leaves, tightly undercurled, of an unusual khaki green, yellow on the undersides. The flowers are starry and grayish white, borne in clusters at the stem tips and resembling those of tree heaths (*see p.59*). The scent of its flowers and foliage, especially noticeable in hot weather, is peculiar; it could perhaps be described as a mixture of honey and warm strawberry jam. It can be grown in most soils, and it prefers a hot, dry spot. A naturally compact shrub, it requires little or no pruning. *O. rosmarinifolius* (Z8–9) is less hardy, but taller (to 10ft/3m) and has lovely grayish green, rosemary-like foliage. '**Silver Jubilee**' has an especially beautiful silver sheen to its leaves and looks at home in Mediterranean-style gardens and plantings.

PRUNUS   Z below

The evergreens are large, robust, useful shrubs, tolerant of pruning and thus good for screening plants or informal hedging. Their leaves remain a good, dark green throughout winter; in spring, the branches are covered with erect spikes of white flowers. *P. laurocerasus* (Z6–9), the cherry laurel, will grow to up to 20ft/6m tall in sun or shade and is suited to any soil except shallow, poor alkaline ones. Prune it after flowering, if necessary. If you are trying to keep hedges reasonably compact, you can also prune lightly in early spring and autumn. There is a dwarf form, '**Otto Luyken**' (*below*), only 3ft/1m high and good *en masse* as a shrubby groundcover, with branches ascending at oblique angles. *P. lusitanica* (Z7–9) (Portuguese laurel) tolerates alkaline soil. It can be pruned closely and often to produce topiary-like shapes, though this means losing the flowers.

OSMANTHUS DELAVAYI

OZOTHAMNUS LEDIFOLIUS

PRUNUS LAUROCERASUS '*OTTO LUYKEN*'

SKIMMIA   Z below

The male and female flowers are usually borne on separate plants, and where both grow together, the females will develop red berries. They grow in most soils, in sun or shade.

There are several types of *S. japonica* (Z7–9), all with white flowers, which in 'Fragrans' are scented. 'Bronze Knight' (*below*) is a male form, no more than 5ft/ 1.5m tall, with flower buds of deep bronze that form in clusters in winter. Set against female plants with red berries, they really brighten up winter gloom. 'Rubella' is another fine male form. The subspecies *reevesiana* will flower and fruit if grown alone, since male and female flowers develop on the same plant, making it an excellent choice for a small garden or a pot (*see p.76*). *S.* × *confusa* 'Kew Green' (Z6–9) is male, with scented cream flowers. These plants are naturally neat, but if long stems spoil the shape, cut them back well to within the bush.

SKIMMIA JAPONICA
'BRONZE KNIGHT'

ZENOBIA   Z5–8

Zenobia pulverulenta (*below*) is the only species, a spreading shrub to 6½ft/2m tall, with thin, irregular, arching stems. Both the shoots and leaves are covered in a white bloom, which fades with age. It flowers in summer, bearing dangling clusters of waxy white bells very similar to the flowers of lily-of-the-valley; they look especially pretty against the white bloom of the new growth. It grows best in neutral to acidic conditions, disliking alkaline soil, and enjoys fertile, organic soil, so add plenty of organic matter – especially leafmold – when planting, and it will tolerate quite dry spells in summer. It thrives in light shade and gives a fresh summer look among spring-flowering woodland shrubs such as rhododendrons (*see p.58*). Prune after flowering to neaten its shape, if desired. It may lose its leaves in hard winters but will survive.

ZENOBIA PULVERULENTA

MORE CHOICES

Calluna (*see p.56*)
Carpenteria (*see p.63*)
Ceanothus, some (*see p.63*)
Cistus (*see p.70*)
Daphne (*see p.53*)
Erica (*see p.56*)
Fatsia (*see p.64*)
Hebe (*see p.67*)
Kalmia (*see p.57*)
Lavandula (*see p.53*)
Leptospermum (*see p.68*)
Olearia (*see p.68*)
Phlomis (*see p.72*)
Pieris (*see p.59*)
Pyracantha (*see p.61*)
Rhododendron, many (*see p.58*)
Rosmarinus (*see p.72*)
Sarcococca (*see p.54*)
Senecio (*see p.76*)
Vaccinium (*see p.59*)
Vinca (*see p.65*)
Yucca (*see p.72*)

Abelia × *grandiflora* (Z6–9)
To 10ft/3m tall, with arching branches and *Weigela*-like flowers (*see p.45*). For full sun.

× *Fatshedera lizei* (Z8–10)
Hybrid between *Fatsia* (*see p.64*) and *Hedera* (ivy); similar to *Fatsia*, enjoying the same conditions. Pollution tolerant; good for gardens where there is not much light. To 6½ft/2m tall and 10ft/3m wide.

Viburnum (*see also p.55*)
Evergreen viburnums include *V. davidii* (Z8–9) (*see p.15*), to 5ft/1.5m tall and (twice the size) *V. tinus* (Z8–10) (laurustinus), both dense and bushy with white flower clusters in late spring and late winter respectively, and blue-black fruits. For sun or shade.

SHRUBS FOR FRAGRANCE

CALYCANTHUS   Z6–9

Known as California allspice, *Calycanthus occidentalis* (*below*) has large, handsome, pointed leaves, green and smooth beneath, and grows up to 6½ft/2m wide and high. It is a sun-loving, deciduous shrub with conspicuous red-brown flowers in summer and early autumn. The flowers are spidery and have a curiously pleasant fragrance of ripe fruit, and the foliage when crushed (or the bark when scratched) has a sweet, spicy aroma that gives the plant its common name. As with many aromatic shrubs, the scent is stronger in full sun.

Calycanthus can be grown in any well-drained, fertile soil. An interesting shrub but not spectacular, it is best blended in with others; many *Prunus* (*see p.43*) and *Viburnum* (*p.45*) enjoy the same conditions.

CHIMONANTHUS   Z7–9

Chimonanthus praecox, or wintersweet, grows up to 8ft/ 2.5m tall and is similar in its foliage to *Calycanthus* (*left*) which belongs to the same family. It has small, stemless, spidery and waxy cream flowers with purple stains at their centers (*see p.10*), borne in late winter on the leafless branches. They have a sweet, spicy fragrance. It needs a sheltered, sunny spot where marginally hardy; otherwise, flowers may not be produced. Although the flowers are borne in late winter, they will resist quite severe cold. Wintersweet can be grown in any well-drained soil including alkaline. There are two forms with finer flowers, '**Grandiflorus**' (*below*), with larger leaves, and **var.** *luteus*, which flowers later in the season, its outer petals of a clear light yellow.

CLETHRA   Z below

Known as sweet pepperbush or summersweet, *Clethra alnifolia* (Z3–9) grows more or less upright to 8ft/2.5m tall. Shoots bear terminal clusters of small, fragrant white flowers in summer. '**Rosea**' has pink flowers, and '**Hummingbird**' grows to only 3ft/1m. Another species from China, C. *barbinervis* (Z6–8), enjoys the same kind of conditions. It is slightly more showy than C. *alnifolia* but is more vulnerable to damage by late spring frosts.

Clethra prefer an acidic, moisture-retentive soil. They can be grown in quite wet ground if necessary, in full sun or partial shade. Since they flower in summer on the current season's growth they can be pruned hard in early spring, or you can simply remove their fading seedheads to encourage more vigor.

CALYANTHUS OCCIDENTALIS

CHIMONANTHUS PRAECOX '*GRANDIFLORUS*'

CLETHRA ALNIFOLIA

DAPHNE Z below

Several daphnes are intensely fragrant. Many are difficult to propagate and are therefore quite hard to come by. They can be fussy in the garden, too. Most enjoy good soil, including alkaline soil, that is moisture-retentive but well drained, and should be grown in full sun to flower well. Do not prune unless absolutely necessary. *Daphne* × *burkwoodii* (Z5–8) *(see p.23)*, to 5ft/1.5m tall, is one of the easiest to grow, especially 'Somerset' *(below)* and 'Carol Mackie', with variegated leaves. *D. bholua* (Z8–9) is deciduous or semi-evergreen, up to 6½ft/2m tall, with stout, erect branches bearing small clusters of exquisitely fragrant white flowers, pink-purple in bud, in late winter into early spring, depending on the climate. They are followed by black berries. *D. cneorum* (Z5–7) is prostrate, with dark pink flowers. *D. collina*, *D. retusa* and *D. tangutica* (all Z7–9) are small evergreens.

HAMAMELIS Z5–9

Hamamelis × *intermedia* 'Jelena' *(below)* is a superb winter-flowering witch hazel of spreading habit, over 10ft/3m high and up to 13ft/4m wide, with hazel-like leaves and strongly fragrant yellow and coppery red flowers. The flowers, which have four threadlike petals, are very cold-tolerant, appearing between midwinter and early spring along the leafless twigs. The leaves often color attractively in autumn. Witch hazels prefer acidic to neutral soil with plenty of organic matter. Although happy in full sun, they are usually seen at their best in light woodland. Pruning is not usually necessary unless branches are badly misplaced and is best done in early spring. If you prefer yellow flowers, perhaps the finest of all *Hamamelis* is 'Pallida' *(see p.15)* for the size and scent of its flowers and their light yellow color.

LAVANDULA Z5–8

Lavenders are wonderful small shrubs for mixing in borders or edging formal and herb beds. They grow well in containers, too *(see p.76)*. The leaves are gray-green. Long stalks are topped by flower clusters in blues, mauves, white, or pink in midsummer. Regular light pruning is essential to keep lavenders bushy. Trim after flowering to remove flower stalks and clip over to the base of the last season's growth in early spring *(see p.35)*. Pruning harder may kill older plants. They are best in full sun in well-drained neutral or limy soils that do not dry out too much. *L. angustifolia* is the classic English lavender. 'Munstead' is compact, while 'Hidcote' is popular for its lovely dark flower color, but is not very robust. *L.* × *intermedia* 'Grappenhall' is large and vigorous. French lavender, *L. stoechas* *(see p.76)*, is less hardy (Z8–9).

DAPHNE × *BURKWOODII* 'SOMERSET'

HAMAMELIS × *INTERMEDIA* 'JELENA'

LAVANDULA ANGUSTIFOLIA; 'NANA ALBA' IN FOREGROUND

LONICERA　Z below

Although many of the climbing honey-suckles are fragrant, only a few shrubby ones are. *L.* × *purpusii* (Z7–9) is one of the best: a hybrid between *L. fragrantissima* (*below*) and *L. standishii*, it is free-flowering and vigorous. They are wide-spreading, graceful shrubs, up to 6½ft/2m tall, that produce small, deliciously scented flowers in late winter on their leafless branches. They can be grown in any well-drained, fertile soil in sun or partial shade. Other shrubby *Lonicera* include *L. syringantha* (Z5–8), intricately branched, with small sea green leaves and lilac-colored flowers in spring. *L. tatarica* (Z3–9) is not as heavily scented; **'Arnold Pink'** has rich pink flowers and red berries. Prune these winter- and spring-flowering honeysuckles after flowering, to shape and to remove old and unproductive wood.

PHILADELPHUS　Z5–8

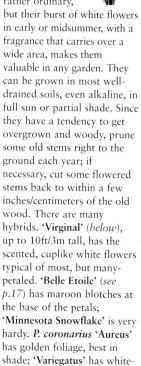

The foliage of *Philadelphus*, or mock orange, is rather ordinary, but their burst of white flowers in early or midsummer, with a fragrance that carries over a wide area, makes them valuable in any garden. They can be grown in most well-drained soils, even alkaline, in full sun or partial shade. Since they have a tendency to get overgrown and woody, prune some old stems right to the ground each year; if necessary, cut some flowered stems back to within a few inches/centimeters of the old wood. There are many hybrids. **'Virginal'** (*below*), up to 10ft/3m tall, has the scented, cuplike white flowers typical of most, but many-petaled. **'Belle Etoile'** (*see p.17*) has maroon blotches at the base of the petals; **'Minnesota Snowflake'** is very hardy. *P. coronarius* **'Aureus'** has golden foliage, best in shade; **'Variegatus'** has white-edged leaves.

SARCOCOCCA　Z6–9

Sarcococca confusa (*below*) is a typical Christmas box, an attractive small evergreen to about 3ft/1m, with small creamy white flowers in winter. Although almost hidden among the foliage, they carry the sweetest and most pervasive fragrance and are followed by black berries in late summer. The small, pointed, glossy leaves make a neat bush, best grown in partial shade on any well-drained soil. The soil can be acidic or limy and, once the plant is established, quite dry. Sometimes grown as informal low hedging, *Sarcococca* can be pruned in early spring to help maintain a good shape.

Other species have similar flowers. *S. hookeriana* has more upright, narrow growth although **var.** *humilis* is low-growing; **'Purple Stem'** has richly tinted young shoots. *S. ruscifolia* is taller but not as hardy (Z8–9).

LONICERA FRAGRANTISSIMA

PHILADELPHUS 'VIRGINAL'

SARCOCOCCA CONFUSA

SYRINGA Z4–8

The common garden lilac, *S. vulgaris*, is a large shrub or even a small tree, growing up to 20ft/6m tall. The flowers are produced in dense sprays in spring and are sweetly scented. Lilacs are happy in most soils, especially alkaline, and flower best in full sun. Pruning consists of removing spent flowerheads and old wood immediately after flowering. You can also prune hard to a stump to renovate lilacs; regrowth is vigorous, but there may be no flowers for a year or two. Flower color ranges mostly from white and cream through classic mauves to red-purple. 'Katherine Havemeyer' (lavender-purple), 'Madame Lemoine' (*below*), 'Charles Joly' (dark purple-red), and 'Primrose' (pale yellow) are among the most popular. For the smaller garden try *S.* × *persica, S. pubescens* subsp. *microphylla,* or *S. meyeri* 'Palibin', often grown in containers (*see p.77*).

SYRINGA VULGARIS 'MADAME LEMOINE'

VIBURNUM Z below

The fragrant viburnums are superb garden plants. *V.* × *bodnantense* 'Dawn' (Z7–8) (*below*) is a fine, upright shrub that can flower from autumn to early spring. Growing up to 10ft/3m tall, the branches arch out when mature, and the old wood bears many small clusters of sweetly scented, rose-tinted flowers. The flower buds are remarkably cold tolerant, but if damaged, more will open. One of its parents, *V. farreri* (Z6–8), is very similar but has smaller flowers. *V.* × *burkwoodii* (Z4–8) is semi-evergreen with shiny leaves and white flowerheads from pink buds in early spring. *V. carlesii* (Z5–8) and *V.* × *juddii* (Z5–9) flower a little later, with a scent reminiscent of old-fashioned carnations. All are suitable for most fertile soils, in sun or partial shade. To prune, cut 2–3 old stems to the base after flowering to encourage new growth.

VIBURNUM × *BODNANTENSE* 'DAWN'

MORE CHOICES

FRAGRANT FLOWERS

Abelia × *grandiflora* (*see p.51*)

Berberis darwinii, B. × *stenophylla* (*see p.46*)

Buddleja davidii (*see p.40*), or try the more unusual *B. globosa,* a large shrub with spherical clusters of orange-yellow, honeyed flowers. Unlike *B. davidii,* it is not pruned hard.

Choisya ternata (*see p.47*)

Cytisus battandieri, C. × *praecox* (*see p.71*)

Elaeagnus angustifolia (*see p.74*), *E.* × *ebbingei* (*see p.47*)

Erica arborea (*see p.59*)

Itea ilicifolia (*see p.49*)

Magnolia grandiflora (*see p.61*)

Mahonia (*see p.49*)

Osmanthus (*see p.50*)

Ozothamnus ledifolius (*see p.50*)

Perovskia atriplicifolia (*see p.72*)

Prunus mume (*see p.43*)

Rhododendron (*see p.58*): deciduous azaleas such as *R. arborescens, R. viscosum,* and hybrids, including the Exbury types; fragrant evergreens include the Loderi group, such as 'King George', and hybrids of *R. decorum.*

Ribes odoratum (*see p.44*)

Skimmia japonica 'Fragrans' (*see p.51*)

Spartium junceum (*see p.69*)

FRAGRANT FOLIAGE

Cistus ladanifer, C. × *cyprius* (*see p.70*)

Escallonia (*see p.48*)

Rosmarinus officinalis (*see p.73*)

Santolina chamaecyparissus (*see p.73*)

SHRUBS FOR ACIDIC SOIL

CALLUNA Z5-7

Heather or ling, **Calluna vulgaris**, is a dense, evergreen, ground-covering dwarf shrub with small stems covered in tiny bell flowers in late summer. *Calluna* prefer acidic but well-drained, light soils. On rich soils they grow vigorously; on poorer soils they are more compact. Best in full sun, they are useful gap-fillers. In sandy soils, the stems, if buried, will root to stabilize banks and slopes. They grow well in containers. Old flowering stems may be trimmed after flowering, although some have seedheads and foliage that are attractive during winter; delay pruning these until early spring. There are hundreds to choose from, with white, pink, or crimson flowers, and many with bright foliage: gold, silver, or reddish bronze. The latter are excellent providers of winter color.

CORYLOPSIS Z below

The only species that dislikes limy soils, **C. pauciflora** (Z6–9) (*below*) is one of the best – densely branched, deciduous, up to 6½ft/2m tall with slender stems, for semi-shade or light woodland. Its leaves are hazel-like and pink-red as they emerge in spring. The early spring flowers are catkinlike, primrose yellow, and lightly fragrant. The flowers and young growth are prone to frost damage. Young growth is also prone to scorch in hot sun. Pruning is unnecessary if plants have room for their graceful habit to develop. Other species tolerate some alkalinity, given deep soil. **C. glabrescens** and **C. sinensis** (both Z6–9) are broader-growing. **C. sinensis** 'Spring Purple' has coppery purple young leaves. **C. 'Winterthur'** (Z5–8) bears bright yellow flowers.

ENKIANTHUS Z5-8

Enkianthus campanulatus (*below*) is a distinctive, deciduous shrub up to 10ft/3m tall, with upright branches and leaves arranged in whorls that take on exquisite colorings in autumn. A lovely plant to grow with other woodlanders such as *Corylopsis*, magnolias, and camellias, it thrives in moisture-retentive, organic soil under trees, or in full sun in cooler areas. The flowers are bell-like, carried in drooping clusters on the previous season's growth in late spring amid emerging foliage. The flowers can vary from greenish cream to rich bronze; although they are somewhat subdued in their coloring, their poise makes them curious and charming. Do not prune unless you need to remove old and dead wood, in which case prune in early spring.

CALLUNA VULGARIS 'ANTHONY DAVIS'

CORYLOPSIS PAUCIFLORA

ENKIANTHUS CAMPANULATUS

ERICA   Z below

Erica has given its name to the heath and heather family (Ericaceae), which includes rhododendrons, azaleas, cranberries, mountain laurel, and blueberries. *Erica carnea* (Z5–7) is the most familiar, a dwarf evergreen shrub with rosy red flowers in late winter and early spring, forming dense mounds and spreading mats. Best grown in full sun or partial shade in light, acidic soils, it tolerates neutral soil if you add plenty of leafmold or other organic matter. There are numerous heathers, two of the most popular being **'Springwood White'** and **'Springwood Pink'**. **'Vivellii'** (*below*) is covered in vivid carmine flowers, with tiny green leaves turning a lovely bronze-red in winter. *Erica cinerea* (Z6–8), the bell heather, and *E. vagans* (Z7–9) are also intolerant of limy soils. All make good underplanting for camellias and rhododendrons, and they grow well in containers.

FOTHERGILLA   Z below

Fothergilla major (Z5–7), (*below*) is a slow-growing, rounded shrub, to 8ft/2.5m tall, with rounded hazel-like leaves that turn to conspicuous red and yellow in autumn. Together with witch hazels (*Hamamelis*), which belong to the same family, they provide some of the best leaf color in acidic-soil gardens. With these, *Enkianthus*, and Japanese maples, the autumn garden can rival the spring garden for color. *Fothergilla* bear white bottlebrush-like clusters of flowers just before the leaves emerge in spring. It prefers moist, peaty, acidic soil. As it naturally forms a well-shaped bush, no pruning should be necessary, except to remove any dead or diseased wood as the plant ages. *F. gardenii* (Z5–7) is smaller, to only 3ft/1m high. Its flowers are similar but scented, and **'Blue Mist'** has glaucous gray tints to its foliage.

KALMIA   Z below

The mountain laurel or calico bush, *Kalmia latifolia* (Z5–9), (*below*) can be 33ft/10m tall in its native haunts, but it normally grows to about 10–13ft/3–4m in garden situations. It has bold, laurel-like leaves topped in early summer by clusters of beautiful, star-shaped pink buds, almost like icing on a cake, that open to saucers of white with red spots. Slow sometimes to get established, these enjoy full sun, but in areas with hot, bright summers they flower well in shade. They prefer rich, moisture-retentive soil, tolerating dry conditions only in late summer. They can be pruned after flowering to shape but otherwise need little attention. For stronger flower color try **'Pink Charm'**, deep pink; **'Freckles'** has more pronounced spotting. *K. angustifolia* (Z7–8) is smaller, to 3ft/1m, with narrow leaves and rosy red flowers.

ERICA CARNEA 'VIVELLII'

FOTHERGILLA MAJOR

KALMIA LATIFOLIA

RHODODENDRONS

A very large genus of plants, including those previously and still familiarly called azaleas. There are hundreds of species and thousands of hybrids, many evergreen, varying widely in size, but mostly of bushy habit.

In general they all prefer acidic soils containing plenty of organic matter. They have a fibrous root system, which benefits from a mulch of rotted leaves or compost; do not use spent mushroom soil, which contains lime. A mulch also helps to conserve moisture, which the plants enjoy; *R. viscosum* (Z4–8) will grow even in a swamp. Some will tolerate a reasonable amount of exposure to wind and full sun while others, particularly the large-leaved types, revel in the protective shade of deep-rooted trees. In areas with alkaline soil, rhododendrons and azaleas can be grown in containers filled with an acidic, organic soil mix.

Pruning needs vary. Most should not need pruning, but will flower better the following year if they are deadheaded (*see p.32*). Some, including the Ironclad Hybrids (Z5–8), (*see below*), can be cut back hard if necessary after flowering. Azaleas can be clipped after flowering. Some *Rhododendron*, especially those with smooth and peeling bark, may react badly to being pruned.

Evergreen rhododendrons

These include many choice and fussy collector's plants such as the blue-flowered *R. augustinii*, (Z6–9). *R. auriculatum* (Z6–8), with heavenly, fragrant white blooms, and huge-leaved, cream-flowered *R. sinogrande* (Z8–10). However, *R. catawbiense* (Z4–8) and *R. ponticum* (Z6–9) are both extremely tough species in the group known as the **Ironclad Hybrids**, with a vast range of flower colors: try rose-crimson 'Cynthia', dark crimson 'Lord Roberts', rosy 'Pink Pearl', or the rich purple of 'Purple Splendour'. 'Mrs. G.W. Leak' is pink with dark markings; 'Sappho' is mauve in bud, opening white with dark throats.

Dwarf hybrids

Many of these originate from alpine garden species such as blue *R. impeditum* (Z5–8) or pink *R. williamsianum* (Z7–9). Most have small leaves. 'Blue Diamond' (Z7–9), (*below left*) is easy to grow, up to 5ft/1.5m tall. 'Elizabeth' (*below center*) has tiered branches. The white *R. yakushimanum* (Z5–9), with white-felted young growth, has given rise to a race of new and very hardy dwarf hybrids (*see p.77 for recommendations*). Perfectly rounded shrubs, they are mostly white-flowered, pink in bud.

Deciduous azaleas

Beautiful plants, often scented and with good autumn leaf color. *R. luteum* (Z6–9) has yellow flowers; those of *R. molle* (Z5–9) are orange-red, and *R. viscosum* (Z4–8), pink-tinged white. There are many hybrid groups between them, such as the **Exbury** and **Ghent** hybrids (both Z5–8), characterized by big clusters of large flowers.

Evergreen azaleas

Popular and versatile, these include house plants. Use singly or in mass plantings. They are excellent shrubs for containers (*see p.77 for recommendations*).

RHODODENDRON 'BLUE DIAMOND'

RHODODENDRON 'ELIZABETH'   *RHODODENDRON* 'SAPPHO'

PIERIS Z below

Pieris japonica (Z6–8) is an evergreen with a dense habit and very attractive, rich green, narrow leaves, which emerge a very attractive bronzy red in spring. Especially beautiful is 'Variegata', with cream-edged leaves; a smaller *Pieris*, it is good in containers (*see also p.76*). The lily-of-the-valley-like flower sprays, usually white but pink in the hybrid *P.* 'Flamingo', form in autumn and open either in late winter or early spring, depending on the weather. The foliage and flowers are vulnerable to late spring frosts so, although the plant itself may be hardy, it should be planted in shelter from cold winds and out of frost pockets. *Pieris* prefer acidic soils containing plenty of organic matter, in full sun or partial shade. Some have bright red young foliage, such as 'Forest Flame' (Z6–9) (*see p.16*), or *P. formosa* var. *forrestii* 'Wakehurst' (Z7–9).

VACCINIUM Z below

The cowberry, *V. vitis-idaea*, (Z2–6), (*below*) is a useful *Vaccinium* for the garden, a dwarf evergreen with a creeping, mat-forming habit. The small boxwoodlike leaves are dark, glossy green above and paler beneath. The flowers are held in terminal sprays of tiny white bells in early summer, followed by dark red berries in autumn. *Vaccinium* also includes many popular fruiting shrubs, such as blueberry, cranberry, bilberry, and huckleberry. They mostly prefer moist, acidic soil, some liking highly acidic and very wet conditions, as in a peat bog. They tolerate some shade. They need little pruning except for the highbush blueberry, *V. corymbosum* (Z3–7), a deciduous shrub with fine autumn color that may be trained on a short, clear trunk to make a bush. Pruning can be carried out after flowering, but avoid cutting away any potential fruit.

MORE CHOICES

Amelanchier (*see p.66*)
Clethra (*see p.52*)
Colutea arborescens (*see p.67*)
Fatsia japonica ♀ (*see p.64*)
Hamamelis (*see p.53*)
Hydrangea macrophylla, *H. quercifolia* ♀ (*see pp.42, 64*)
Magnolia many (*see p.61*)
Skimmia (*see p.51*)

Erica arborea (Z9–10)
The tree heath is similar-looking in its foliage and flowers to other *Erica* (*see p.57*) but on a much bigger scale, growing up to 20ft/6m tall and developing thick, woody branches. Its white spring flowers are borne in fragrant cones on green, upright shoots. Unlike small heaths, tree heaths can be cut very hard back if necessary, after flowering.

Arctostaphylos uva-ursi (Z2–6)
The red bearberry, closely related to *Vaccinium* (*left*), is another very low-growing evergreen that makes an effective groundcover, even in very sandy, dry soils. It has small white flowers and red berries.

The following tolerate acidic soils if the pH is above 5.5:
Cotoneaster (*see pp.47, 60*)
Cytisus (*see p.71*)
Elaeagnus (*see p.47*)
Hypericum (*see p.49*)
Philadelphus (*see p.54*)
Pyracantha (*see p.61*)
Syringa (*see p.55*)
Viburnum (*see pp.45, 55*)
Weigela (*see p.45*)

PIERIS FORMOSA VAR. FORRESTII

VACCINIUM VITIS-IDAEA SUBSP. MINUS

SHRUBS FOR WALL-TRAINING

CEANOTHUS   Z9–10

Normally growing up to 10–13ft/ 3-4m, evergreen *Ceanothus* (California lilac) are either upright or prostrate shrubs, mainly blue-flowered and among the finest wall shrubs for areas that do not suffer from harsh winters. The small evergreen leaves are held close to the stems; above them are carried small, dense balls of tiny flowers, of an especially rich dark blue in 'Concha' (*below*). Other good blue ceanothus include **C. x veitchianus**, 'Trewithen Blue', 'Millerton Point', 'Yankee Point', and 'Cascade'; for white flowers, choose 'Snow Flurries'. If grown untrained they need plenty of room and strong supports to hold their weight. Prune after flowering, cutting back flowered shoots no thicker than a pencil. Do not prune back into old bare wood; it will not reshoot.

CHAENOMELES   Z5–8

Sometimes known as japonicas, these are useful wall shrubs for cold areas. *C. speciosa* types, vigorous shrubs up to 8ft/2.5m tall, are the most suitable for training. The species is red-flowered, with small cup-shaped flowers in late winter and early spring, but there are other colors; in 'Moerloosei' (often labeled as 'Apple Blossom') they are especially pretty, white on the outside and deep pink inside. The flowers are carried on the previous season's growth. Prune wall-trained plants twice a year to encourage the buildup of flowering spurs (*see p.37*) close to the main branches, close to the wall. First shorten the long summer shoots by two-thirds in midsummer, then shorten these growths again in late winter to three or four buds.

COTONEASTER   Z5–7

Small-leaved cotoneasters that carry their branches in flat fan arrangements or "fishbone" shapes, for example *C. horizontalis* and *C. divaricatus* (*below and p.21*), make low-growing shrubs, often used as a groundcover, but are also excellent for wall-training in sun or shade, in many climates and most soils. They need very little pruning, simply encouragement, guiding stems to supports to grow flat up against a wall, where they can reach 6½–10ft/2–3m. The small white flowers open from pink buds in spring and are followed by red berries in autumn, which can persist well into winter: a fine sight among the leaves as they turn red in autumn. Pruning can be carried out after flowering or in late winter but should rarely be necessary.

CEANOTHUS 'CONCHA'

CHAENOMELES SPECIOSA 'MOERLOOSEI'

COTONEASTER DIVARICATUS

MAGNOLIA   Z7–9

Magnolia grandiflora is not as slow to grow and flower as some other magnolias. In its native southern US, this magnificent evergreen reaches treelike proportions. It can be grown as a large shrub or trained against a house wall, where in marginal areas it benefits from the shelter and extra warmth. The flowers in late summer and autumn are spectacular: large, creamy white, with a hypnotic fragrance; a single one can scent an entire room. It has handsome, large, shiny green leaves, shorter and broader in '**Goliath**' (*below*) and narrower in '**Exmouth**'; '**Ferruginea**' has more rusty hairiness under the leaf. *M. grandiflora* '**Edith Bogue**' is considered among the hardiest. All are happy in almost any soil, including fairly alkaline ones, as long as it is deep and fertile. Prune in early spring or autumn to train to the wall (*see p.37*).

PYRACANTHA   Z below

Easily grown in most soil types, in sun or shade, these are very useful shrubs for wall-training; they can be pruned to keep a dense habit and still flower well, which makes them very suitable for intruder-proof flowering hedging. Deciduous, with sharply thorny stems and bunches of brilliantly colored berries in autumn, they are also known as firethorns. They bear clusters of white flowers in spring. They are large shrubs, up to 16ft/5m tall when freestanding, that need sturdy support for wall-training, such as a frame of wooden slats. The young stems are flexible and can be trained horizontally to go around windows and doors.
P. '**Watereri**' (Z7–9), (*below*) is good for walls, as are *P. rogersiana* (Z8–9) with orange fruits (yellow in '**Flava**'); '**Teton**' (Z6–9), with an erect habit and orange fruits, and '**Sparkler**' (Z7–9), with cream leaf margins.

MORE CHOICES

Other shrubs for wall-training, many of which benefit from the protection of a wall where marginally hardy, include:
Chimonanthus (*see p.52*)
Cotoneaster conspicuus '**Decorus**', *C. microphyllus* (*see p.48*) Will need regular clipping to keep them flat and dense
Forsythia suspensa (*see p.41*)
Fuchsia magellanica (*see p.41*)
Garrya (*see p.48*)
Itea ilicifolia (*see p.49*)
Olearia macrodonta (*see p.68*)
Prunus cistena, P. mume, P. triloba (*see p.43*)
Stachyurus (*see p.65*); S. '**Magpie**' is especially pretty wall-trained
Viburnum macrocephalum (*see p.45*)

Alternatives to *Buddleja davidii* (*see p.40*) ideal for walls, similar-looking but less hardy and more delicate in flower and leaf, are *Buddleja crispa* (Z8–9), up to 6½ft/2m tall, with heavily white-felted stems and leaves and purple-pink flowers, ideal as a backdrop to a white or silver planting design; and *Buddleja* × *colvilei* '**Kewensis**' (Z8–9), a much larger shrub up to 13ft/4m tall, with large, drooping spires of fragrant, pink-red flowers in spring. Both prefer a sunny position in well-drained soil. Unlike *B. davidii*, they should not be pruned hard; prune *B. crispa* lightly in early spring, and '**Kewensis**' after flowering.

MAGNOLIA GRANDIFLORA 'GOLIATH'

PYRACANTHA 'WATEŘERI'

WALL SHRUBS FOR MILD AREAS

ABUTILON   Z8–10

Hardy only in zones 8–10, these can be grown as freestanding shrubs elsewhere, but their slender stems make them prone to flopping over, so tying them into a wired wall gives them support as well as providing shelter and reflected warmth where needed.
A. megapotamicum (*below*), up to 8ft/2.5m tall, has small, arrow-shaped, dark green leaves, marked with cream in 'Variegatum'. It needs moisture-retentive soil in full sun. In mild areas the flowers can be carried at almost any time of year, but mostly during summer and autumn. Although the flowers are not large individually, the quantity of contrasting red and yellow blooms makes a striking and intriguing display. You can prune in early spring, cutting back hard to the wall, if necessary, to neaten the plant.

AZARA   Z8–10

Azara integrifolia (*below*) is a tall evergreen shrub that in marginal areas must be grown against a wall for protection. *A. microphylla*, to 10–13ft/3–4m tall, has very small leaves and a stiff upright habit. Both this and *A. integrifolia* have good variegated-leaved forms; all have yellow flowers. The leaves are oval and dark green. The flowers are little tassels of yellow stamens borne in early spring, sweetly fragrant. *Azara* tend to form a strong central stem, almost like a small tree, but can be pruned to maintain a denser habit. They can be grown on most soils that are free-draining and are fairly drought-tolerant when established, so they cope well in the rain shadow created by a wall or fence, provided that they have been well cared for when young.

CARPENTERIA   Z8–9

Known as the California orange blossom, *Carpenteria californica* (*below*) is a rounded evergreen shrub, hardy in zones 8–9. Its foliage benefits from the warmth of a wall and additional shelter from cold winds to stop it from becoming bruised and unsightly. The flowers resemble those of its close relative, *Philadelphus*, carried in clusters during summer. Look out for plants with names such as 'Ladhams' Variety', which have reliably good, large flowers. *Carpenteria* also have attractive peeling bark. Grow them freestanding (to about 16ft/5m tall) or loosely tied in against a wall, in almost any well-drained soil; they thrive in sun. Prune lightly after flowering or harder, if needed, in spring; this may be at the expense of some flowers.

ABUTILON MEGAPOTAMICUM

AZARA INTEGRIFOLIA

CARPENTERIA CALIFORNICA

CORONILLA Z below

Known as the scorpion senna, *Coronilla emerus* (Z7–9) (*below*), sometimes also called *Hippocrepis*, is a sun-loving, deciduous member of the pea family that thrives in a sheltered site. Its leaves are divided into tiny round leaflets, and throughout the summer it is covered with small yellow pea flowers tipped with a touch of rusty red. Long, slender seedpods then develop, curved like a scorpion's tail. Up to 6½ft/2m tall and wide, forming a dense thicket of a bush, it can be tied in loosely to a wall to draw it up in height and make it more compact, as well as giving extra shelter. It responds well to pruning in early spring to keep it in shape. In mild climates choose the more attractive but more tender *C. valentina* 'Variegata' (Z8–9) with lovely blue-green leaves edged in cream. Much smaller, it could be grown in a pot and overwintered under cover.

CORONILLA EMERUS

FREMONTODENDRON

Evergreen, or often semi-evergreen, fast-growing shrubs for sheltered and warm gardens in (Z8–10), *Fremonodendron* are easy to train against walls, although you must wear gloves when handling them: the hairs on the stems and leaves irritate some people's skin. They also shed these hairs freely, so beware when gardening beneath them. 'California Glory' (*below*) is the most widely seen; it is a spectacular shrub when in full flower, up to 23ft/7m tall, covered in large, yellow cup-shaped flowers from early summer through autumn. They are not fussy as to soil type, as long as it it free-draining. They do not like being transplanted, however, and it is best to plant a small specimen; once established, it will grow rapidly. Prune the shoot tips to encourage a more bushy habit and to keep the shrub close to the wall.

FREMONTODENDRON 'CALIFORNIA GLORY'

MORE CHOICES

These shrubs are also only for mild and warm-climate regions, unless they can be given a very favorable spot, such as a sunny house wall or courtyard garden. In cool climates they make good conservatory plants.

Callistemon (*see p.46*)
Grevillea (*see p.48*)

Acacia dealbata (Z9–10)
Best in warm-climate gardens, where it can grow into a 100ft/30m-tall tree, and worth trying with the protection of a wall in mild areas. The fluffy sprays of tiny yellow flowers in early spring are very fragrant. Even where they are not reliably produced, the shrub is beautiful for its feathery, gray-blue foliage alone. *A. baileyana* (Z10–11) is smaller; its foliage has a slight purple tinge to it.

Piptanthus nepalensis (Z9–10)
A semi-evergreen, vigorous shrub up to 13ft/4m tall, with three-lobed dark green leaves and spikes of bright yellow pea flowers in early summer. Grown in full sun in any fertile soil, it thrives in milder areas or with the protection of a wall. Flowering on the previous season's growth, it should be pruned after flowering.

Plumbago auriculata (Z9–10)
Sprawling deciduous shrub that needs support, with showers of lovely pale blue flowers throughout summer. Against a wall, it may reach 13–16ft/4–5m; in a pot in full sun, about 3ft/1m. Prune in early spring to encourage new growth.

SHRUBS FOR SHADE

CAMELLIA   Z7–8

*Camellia ×
williamsii* is a
hybrid group
with many good
qualities. A bit
hardier than *C. japonica* (*see
p.46*), the smaller evergreen
leaves are more pointed. The
habit is more lax, and the
flowers are produced over a
longer season. The flower buds
are prone to damage from
hard and late frosts; a shady
position is ideal to protect
them from too-rapid thawing
in early morning sun. Blooms
may open in early winter and
sporadically until spring. In
colder areas they flower
mostly in early spring. All
camellias prefer an acidic soil
with plenty of organic matter,
such as leafmold, added. In
dappled shade or against a
wall they can reach up to
10ft/3m. Among the finest
are '**Donation**' (silver-pink,
semidouble flowers), '**J.C.
Williams**' (pale pink), and
'**Francis Hanger**' (*below*).

FATSIA   Z8–10

Grown
chiefly for
its leathery,
deeply lobed,
large evergreen
leaves, *Fatsia japonica*, a
relative of English ivy, has
ivylike, greenish cream
"drumstick" flowerheads in
autumn (*below*). These are
often damaged by frosts, but
if they remain unscathed,
large bunches of black berries
develop. Needing some shelter
for its large leaves, this thrives
in most soils and, like ivy, in
quite heavy shade, reaching
up to 10ft/3m.

This shrub evokes a tropical
or subtropical effect,
combining well with plants
such as bamboo and tree
ferns, which also do well in
sheltered moist shade.
'**Variegata**' has creamy white
splashes on the leaves. If
Fatsia grow too large they can
be pruned as hard as you like,
in early spring before the new
shoots emerge.

HYDRANGEA   Z7–9

All hydrangeas (*see also p.42*)
will grow in shade, but some
are especially
suited to it.
H. aspera is
one of these, and the lovely
Villosa Group (*below*) has the
best flowers, plus long,
velvety leaves and peeling,
gray-brown papery bark. The
large flowerheads have a ring
of lacy, rose-lilac florets
surrounding a boss of minute,
rich blue flowers. Unlike other
hydrangeas, if flower buds are
damaged by late spring frosts,
more shoots grow to put on
the late summer show. It is
happy in any rich, cool soil, in
the dappled shade of trees or
shaded by a building, growing
up to 13ft/4m tall and often
much wider. It can be pruned
in late winter, quite hard if
needed. For a smaller shrub,
shade-loving *H. quercifolia*
grows to about 6½ft/2m tall,
with cones of white florets and
oaklike leaves that take on
good autumn color.

CAMELLIA × WILLIAMSII
'FRANCIS HANGER'

FATSIA JAPONICA

HYDRANGEA ASPERA
VILLOSA GROUP

STACHYURUS Z7–9

Stachyurus praecox (*below*) is an elegant, fairly upright deciduous shrub, to 8ft/2.5m tall, with deep wine-red stems that contrast perfectly with the small, rounded, pale yellow flowers that hang in catkins off the leafless stems in late winter. *Stachyurus* will grow on any lime-free soil, but if there is plenty of organic matter in it they tolerate more alkaline conditions. They are best grown in shade where the early flowers and leaves will be more protected from frost. Pruning is usually unnecessary unless a branch spoils the shape or becomes very old and unproductive. The best time to prune is in early spring after flowering. *S. chinensis* differs little from *S. praecox* except that its stems are not red-tinted, and it has slightly longer flower tassels. The beautiful, variegated cultivar 'Magpie' has leaves splashed creamy white with pink around their margins.

STACHYURUS PRAECOX

VINCA Z below

Periwinkles, which give their name to the piercing blue of their flowers, are trailing evergreen shrubs that form a ground-covering carpet by means of spreading roots and arching stems that root as they touch the ground. Flowers open along the stems during spring and early summer, with a few carried on into the autumn. The greater periwinkle, *V. major* (Z7–11) can be very invasive, even in its variegated form, but *V. minor* (Z4–9), the lesser periwinkle (*below*), is a useful plant for shade in most soil types and will, once established, tolerate quite dry conditions. Although it grows in heavy shade, it flowers best in dappled shade. Every few years it is worth cutting the whole plant down to the ground to encourage fresh new growth. This is best done after the first flush of flowers in spring. There are periwinkles with variegated leaves and with white, pink, purple, or double flowers.

VINCA MINOR

MORE CHOICES

Chaenomeles (see p.40)
Choisya (see p.75)
Corylopsis (see p.56)
Cotoneaster (see pp.47, 60)
Daphne, especially evergreens such as *D. laureola (see p.53)*
Deutzia (see p.40)
Elaeagnus × ebbingei, E. pungens (see p.47)
Enkianthus (see p.56)
Erica (see p.56)
Forsythia (see p.41)
Fothergilla (see p.48)
Garrya (see p.48)
Hamamelis (see p.53)
Hypericum (see p.49)
Kalmia (see p.57)
Kerria japonica (see p.42)
Magnolia (see p.61)
Mahonia (see p.49)
Nandina domestica (see p.45)
Osmanthus delavayi, O. × burkwoodii, O. heterophyllus (see p.50)
Pieris (see p.59)
Philadelphus (see p.54)
Pyracantha (see p.61)
Rhododendron, including azaleas *(see p.58)*
Ribes sanguineum, R. odoratum (see p.44)
Sarcococca (see p.54)
Skimmia (see p.51)
Vaccinium (see p.59)
Viburnum × burkwoodii, V. carlesii (see p.55), V. davidii (see p.51)
Weigela (see p.45)

SHRUBS FOR EXPOSED SITES

AMELANCHIER   Z3–7

Amelanchier canadensis (*below*) is a large deciduous shrub, sometimes a small tree, with beautiful young foliage that unfurls with a pinkish tinge very early in the spring, at the same time as clusters of white flowers open. Often trained to a single stem, it actually grows naturally as a multistemmed shrub. It can reach 20–23ft/ 6–7m in height. In autumn, the foliage takes on lovely, clear shades of red and pink.

Amelanchier thrive in most soils that are not too limy and, although growing well in well-drained soil, will tolerate almost boglike conditions. Although they grow in woodlands they also grow well in very exposed situations and can withstand salt-laden winds. Prune to shape, if necessary, and remove old or dead wood in late winter.

BERBERIS   Z5–8

B. thunbergii and its many forms are easy to grow in almost all soils in full sun, except for **'Aurea'**, whose golden foliage tends to burn in hot sun. They are dense, very thorny, rounded shrubs with small leaves. The early-summer flowers are pale yellow, hanging in small clusters, followed by bright red berries in autumn. The form *atropurpurea* (*below*) has dark coppery purple leaves that turn wine-red in autumn. Some varieties have been bred for a compact or upright habit, ideal for hedges – either low for borders, or up to 8ft/2.5m tall for impenetrable boundary screens, useful to protect other plants in cold windy sites. The thorns can make pruning difficult, but hard pruning and shearing may be carried out in late winter and after flowering.

BRACHYGLOTTIS   Z9–10

'Sunshine' (*below*) is a very popular "ever-gray" shrub with silvery leaves, forming a dense mound up to 3ft/1m high and more across. Bright yellow flowers open from clusters of silvery white buds; when in full flower the shrub is quite spectacular.

B. monroi has smaller, wavy-edged leaves, not as silver, but is equally good in flower. Like many silver-leaved plants, they prefer full sun in well-drained soil. They tolerate mild winds and sea spray. They make good companions for *Olearia* (*next page*) and *Hebe* (*facing page*), which enjoy similar conditions. Pruning simply consists of removing spent flowerheads to encourage a compact habit. Old or untrimmed straggly plants that have opened up can be pruned hard after flowering.

AMELANCHIER CANADENSIS

BERBERIS THUNBERGII F. *ATROPURPUREA*

BRACHYGLOTTIS 'SUNSHINE'

COLUTEA   Z6–9

Colutea arborescens (*below*) is a quick-growing shrub, to 10ft/3m tall and wide, with divided leaves on gray shoots and warm yellow flowers throughout the summer. These are followed by inflated seedpods that give it its common name of bladder senna (senna being a name common to yellow-flowered members of the pea family). Ideal for poor soils, on dry sunny banks, and even in polluted areas, it is tough and takes considerable wind exposure. It can become messy but can be pruned hard in early spring, removing old and dead growth at the same time. Hybrids between this species and *C. orientalis*, with brownish red flowers but otherwise similar, include *C. × media* 'Copper Beauty', with unusual coppery flowers. Good companions for *Colutea* include dry soil-loving *Cytisus* and *Cistus* (*pp.70–71*) *Genista* (*right*) and *Tamarix (next page)*.

GENISTA   Z below

Genista is very similar to *Cytisus* (*see p.71*) in many respects; both are known as brooms and prefer a sunny spot in dry areas. Many *Genista*, especially the low-growing types, will take considerable exposure, even to salt-laden winds. They can be grown in most soil types and are fairly lime-tolerant. The only pruning that may be necessary is to trim with shears after flowering to maintain a compact habit. *Genista* are often rather short-lived. *G. pilosa* 'Procumbens' (Z6–9) (*below*) is a dense, ground-hugging shrub forming a mat of gray-green stems smothered with small golden yellow flowers in early summer. Other prostrate brooms include *G. tinctoria* (Z2–8) and double-flowered 'Flore Pleno'. *G. lydia* (Z6–9) grows a little taller. *G. hispanica* (Z7–9) is the toughest, and is prickly and dense. More treelike and less hardy is *G. aetnensis* (Z9–10), the Mount Etna broom.

HEBE   Z8–10

Hebe, almost all from New Zealand, are wind-resistant (including salt winds). They prefer full sun and thrive in any reasonable, well-drained soil, but although they tolerate quite dry conditions for some time, they are not drought-resistant. Pruning is usually not necessary; if you must, always cut stems back to a leafy shoot, not into bare wood. *H. pinguifolia* 'Pagei' is one of the hardiest and makes an excellent groundcover. *H. albicans* (*see p.75*) and purple-tinged 'Red Edge' are slightly taller. The larger-leaved *Hebe* are less hardy but more showy in flower; look out for *H.* 'Midsummer Beauty', with long blue flower spikes and long leaves, 'Great Orme' (*see p.24*) and 'Amy', also called 'Purple Queen', up to 5ft/1.5m tall, with a purplish hue to the leaves harmonizing with the spikes of rosy purple flowers in midsummer.

COLUTEA ARBORESCENS

GENISTA PILOSA 'PROCUMBENS'

HEBE 'AMY'

HIPPOPHAE Z3–8

Although not a showy flowerer, *Hippophae rhamnoides* (*below*), a tall, deciduous, spiny shrub, has beautiful small, narrow, gray leaves, scaly bark, tiny yellow-green flowers in spring, and, on female plants, bright orange-yellow berries in autumn that may persist through winter. It grows up to 13ft/4m tall. Its greatest assets are its tolerance to wind, especially salt winds, and its ability to grow in almost any soil, from very dry to almost boggy. Since male and female flowers are carried on separate plants on *Hippophae*, it is necessary to plant at least one male plant for two or more females to ensure berry production, so these shrubs are ideal for group plantings and shelter hedges. Prune in late winter if necessary to improve the shape, which can become a little ungainly and leggy, cutting back as hard as you like.

LEPTOSPERMUM Z9–10

Leptospermum lanigerum (*below*) is a beautiful, gray-leaved evergreen shrub native to Australia, where it can grow to 13ft/4m tall, flowering in early summer with groups of small white flowers with deep purple markings inside them. These nestle among the silky and hairy young foliage on drooping branches, giving the whole plant an airy grace. *Leptospermum* prefer well-drained, acidic to neutral soil in full sun and will tolerate salt winds and an open position in milder areas. *L. lanigerum* is hardier than most and well worth trying. *L. scoparium*, smaller with green leaves, is more frequently grown but less hardy; look for 'Red Damask', which has long-lasting, double red flowers. Where marginally hardy they will require protection, such as that from a wall. Prune to shape, if desired, in early spring.

OLEARIA Z8–10

Olearia are medium-sized evergreens smothered with white daisylike flowers in early summer. The leaves, small and gray-felted, are soft to touch and aromatic. *Olearia* are best grown in full sun in any well-drained soil and will even thrive on alkaline soil. Although its parents are from Australasia, *O.* × *scilloniensis* (*below*) is from the Scilly Isles, where it must tolerate very strong salt-laden winds. The hardiest *Olearia* is *O.* × *haastii*, which forms a dense hummock, bearing starry white flowers in late summer.

Very tolerant of pruning (in early spring), *Olearia* make ideal hedges and small windbreaks in maritime areas. The larger, holly-leaved *O. macrodonta*, with gray-green leaves, can reach up to 13ft/4m and is ideal for this purpose, while *O.* × *haastii* would make a good low hedge.

HIPPOPHAE RHAMNOIDES

LEPTOSPERMUM LANIGERUM

OLEARIA × SCILLONIENSIS

SPARTIUM   Z8–10

Closely related to both *Cytisus* and *Genista* (*see pp.71, 67*) and known as Spanish broom, **Spartium junceum** (*below*) is a Mediterranean shrub, strong-growing, often leggy in habit, up to 10ft/3m tall, with erect, slender stems and such small leaves as to look almost leafless. The flowers are typical of a broom: large, pealike, and yellow, and borne in terminal clusters in late summer and into autumn, with a wonderfully sweet fragrance. Spanish broom is easily grown and trouble-free, given a sunny position in any well-drained, even poor, soil. Less hardy in colder inland areas, where it can be given the shelter of a wall, it is ideal for mild maritime regions, where its growth is more compact, being kept low and bushy by the sea winds. Like most brooms, it is best trimmed in early spring with shears to prevent it from becoming too straggly.

SPARTIUM JUNCEUM

TAMARIX   Z below

Quite durable and easily grown in any soil type except shallow alkaline soil, tamarisks are excellent plants for windy areas, particularly near the sea, where they happily tolerate salty winds. *T. ramosissima* (Z3–8) (*below* and *p.25*) is a striking shrub for late summer, with feathery, pale gray-green foliage and large, soft pink, airy plumes of flowers that branch and open for many weeks. It looks good growing among or behind tall perennials. Left unpruned it will form an almost treelike shape, often leaning with a lop-sided look. It can also be pruned in early spring to encourage larger flowers and a longer display. *T. tetrandra* (Z5–9) and *T. parviflora* (Z5–8) both flower in early summer, so hard pruning in spring would mean the loss of flowers. The best treatment for these is to prune lightly in summer after flowering, and again in winter.

TAMARIX RAMOSISSIMA

MORE CHOICES

FOR COLD, WINDY GARDENS

Calluna (*see p.56*)
Chaenomeles (*see p.40*)
Erica (*see p.56*)
Kerria japonica (*see p.42*)
Hydrangea paniculata (*see p.42*)
Kalmia (*see p.57*)
Rhododendron Ironclad Hybrids and hybrids of *R. yakushimanum* (*see p.58*)
Spiraea × vanhouttei (*see p.44*)
Syringa vulgaris (*see p.55*)
Vaccinium some (*see p.59*)
Viburnum opulus, *V. dentatum* (*see p.45*)

FOR SEASIDE GARDENS

Buddleja davidii, *B. globosa* (*see pp.40, 55*)
Berberis darwinii (*see p.46*)
Calluna (*see p.56*)
Cistus ladanifer (*see p.70*)
Cotoneaster, all small-leaved types (*see pp.47, 60–61*)
Elaeagnus (*see pp.47, 74*)
Escallonia (*see p.48*)
Fuchsia magellanica (*see p.41*)
Hydrangea macrophylla (*see p.42*)
Lavandula (*see p.53*)
Phlomis (*see p.72*)
Prunus × cistena, *P. maritima* (*see p.43*), also *P. spinosa*
Rosmarinus (*see p.72*)
Santolina (*see p.72*)
Viburnum opulus (*see p.45*)
Yucca (*see p.72*)

Shrubs for Dry Places

CARYOPTERIS — Z6–9

*Caryopteris ×
clandonensis*
(*below*) is a
deciduous
small shrub, to
5ft/1.5m, with aromatic gray-green leaves and little clusters of bright blue flowers in late summer at the tips of stems and in the leaf joints. It blends well with late-flowering perennials and other small gray-leaved shrubs such as lavender and *Perovskia*. Best grown in a sunny site in any well-drained soil, *Caryopteris*, once established, tolerate quite dry conditions. Like other late-flowering shrubs they can be pruned hard in spring: cut stems down to just above new, emerging shoots. 'Heavenly Blue', 'Kew Blue', and 'Fern-down' (*see p.12*) vary in the intensity of blue, but all are recommended. 'Worcester Gold' has yellow-green leaves that contrast strikingly with the blue flowers. All attract butterflies.

CERATOSTIGMA — Z6–9

Ceratostigma
flowers are of
such a true
blue, nearly
cobalt, that
they show up other so-called blue-flowered plants and are best planted among pinks and purples. **C. willmottianum** (*below*) is deciduous, up to 3ft/1m tall, flowering in late summer and into autumn. The leaves take on rich reddish autumn tints, showing off late flowers to even better advantage. In full sun in well-drained soil it becomes quite drought-resistant. It may be cut down by winter cold, but you can prune down to new growth in early spring. This also encourages better flowers. **C. griffithii** is evergreen, denser, more bristly, but not as hardy or showy. **C. plumbaginoides** is hardier, ground-covering, and tolerant of dry shade beneath shrubs, with flame-colored foliage in autumn.

CISTUS — Z below

The sun or
rock roses
are small
evergreens,
up to
5ft/1.5m tall, with grayish foliage and large, wrinkled, papery-looking flowers. Many have blotches on the petals, such as **C. × purpureus** (Z9–10) (*below*). **C. laurifolius** has larger, aromatic leaves and white flowers. Mostly native to Mediterranean regions, *Cistus* are sun-lovers for dry soils of most types, including alkaline. **C. × corbariensis** (Z8–10), with white flowers, is perhaps the hardiest. In general they respond poorly to pruning, but they can be trimmed lightly in early spring, back to new growth, to maintain well-formed bushes. Some, particularly hybrids of **C. ladanifer** (Z8–10), can be leggy; tip-pruning actively growing shoots can help.

CARYOPTERIS × CLANDONENSIS

*CERATOSTIGMA
WILLMOTTIANUM*

CISTUS × PURPUREUS

CYTISUS   Z below

A dense, bushy plant with thin, green twigs, **Cytisus ×** **praecox** (Z6–9) has the best qualities of its parents: compact growth – many *Cytisus* tend to get leggy – and a profusion of fragrant, vivid yellow flowers in early summer. *Cytisus*, or brooms, are best grown on dry, sunny banks, in almost any soil, the poorer the better. They are suitable for windy sites, if staked until established. Brooms are short-lived plants, often not making ten years old, but are fast-growing, to 6½–8ft/ 2–2.5m, and easily replaced. Shear them after flowering to encourage compact growth. Hybrids of the yellow-flowered common broom, **C. scoparius** (Z6–8), often have brightly colored keels to the flowers; look for **C. 'Goldfinch'** in red and yellow, or **'Windlesham Ruby'** (*see p.10*) with flowers of ruby red. **C. × kewensis** (Z6–8) and **C. × beanii** (Z7–8) are excellent prostrate brooms.

HELIANTHEMUM   Z6–8

Forming low evergreen mounds only a few inches/cm high but 3ft/1m or more across, these lovely shrubs have small leaves and in early summer are covered in small, cup-shaped flowers in almost every color except purple and blue, with yellow stamens. Closely related to *Cistus* (*facing page*) and also known as rock roses, *Helianthemum* enjoy the same conditions: full sun and any well-drained soil, including alkaline. Pruning should be unnecessary, but they may be lightly trimmed, removing old flowerheads afer flowering. **'Wisley Pink'** (*below*) and **'Wisley Primrose'**, with lovely pale yellow flowers, are both especially beautiful due to their gray foliage. Other hybrids have green foliage and brightly colored flowers: for example **'Ben Hope'**, carmine and deep orange, **'Amy Baring'**, deep buttercup yellow, and **'Mrs C.W. Earle'**, bright red.

LAVATERA   Z below

The shrubby *Lavatera* are upright plants, 1.5–2m tall, with stiff stems and sage green leaves, flowering, usually in pinks and purples, from mid-summer until autumn. Although short-lived, they grow fast and are easily grown on any well-drained to dry soil, even quite poor ground. They are also excellent in maritime areas, resisting salt winds; they need staking well, however, in exposed positions. In cold winters they will be killed back but can be pruned right down to the new emerging shoots at the base in early spring. Hard pruning also encourages tall, vigorous stems. **'Barnsley'** (Z7–9), (*below*), with light pink cup-shaped flowers with a dark eye, is a sport from **L. olbia**, a good shrub in its own right, as is dark pink **'Rosea'** (Z8–10). The even darker purple-pink **'Burgundy Wine'** (Z8–10) is among the many new *Lavatera* available.

CYTISUS × PRAECOX 'ALLGOLD'

HELIANTHEMUM 'WISLEY PINK'

LAVATERA 'BARNSLEY'

PEROVSKIA   Z6–9

Perovskia atriplicifolia is an upright, grayish white-stemmed shrub, 1–1.5m tall, with spires of lavender-blue flowers throughout late summer. The deeply cut leaves are strongly aromatic. In milder areas it will form a woody framework but in cold areas, even though it is very hardy, the topgrowth will get cut down by cold. You can cut all the stems down hard to new emerging shoots within 6–8in/15–20cm of the ground in the spring. Easily grown in full sun in any well-drained soil, *Perovskia* tolerate very dry conditions and exposure to salt winds. Their gray and blue coloring blends perfectly with other gray-leaved plants, late summer perennials, and ornamental grasses. '**Blue Spire**' (*below*) and the similar '**Superba**' are beautiful hybrids, as is '**Filigran**', with especially finely cut leaves. *P. abrotanoides* is similar but with hairier stems.

PHLOMIS   Z below

Phlomis fruticosa (Z8–9) is a small, rounded evergreen shrub with woolly gray-green leaves and in summer, tall stems of tiered clusters of yellow flowers, followed by attractive seedheads. It is perfect for blending with shrubs of a similar habit and coloring such as *Santolina*. Known as Jerusalem sage, it will grow to about 1.25m tall in any well-drained soil in full sun, tolerating coastal and very dry conditions. Some dislike the yellow flower color; pruning hard in early spring will ensure a mound of foliage and only a few flowers. It is advisable to prune a little every year to maintain a good shape. *P.* '**Edward Bowles**' (Z8–9) has more attractive, paler yellow flowers. Other species include *P. chrysophylla* (Z9–10), similar to *P. fruticosa* but with yellow-tinted leaves. *P. italica* (Z9–10) is smaller with narrow leaves and pink-lilac whorled flowers.

ROSMARINUS   Z8–10

Rosemary (**R.** *officinalis*, *below*) is an upright evergreen, to 2m tall, that sprawls with age. It has narrow gray-green leaves that are strongly aromatic; it is a popular culinary herb. Small, pale blue flowers stud the stems in spring. From the Mediterranean, it thrives in any well-drained soil in full sun. Where not hardy it is best grown in a pot and brought indoors for winter (*see p.76*). In milder areas it can be grown as an informal hedge that can be lightly sheared after flowering. In ideal conditions it may grow up to 6½ft/2m tall, but even '**Miss Jessopp's Upright**' (*see p.24*), one of the most suitable for hedging, tends to splay out unless pruned to maintain its habit. Prostrate types are good over stone retaining walls. '**Severn Sea**' is low-growing, more tender but with brighter blue flowers in summer. There are also rosemaries with white and pink flowers.

PEROVSKIA '*BLUE SPIRE*'

PHLOMIS FRUTICOSA

ROSMARINUS OFFICINALIS

SANTOLINA   Z below

Santolina pinnata (Z9–10), (*below*) is the best lavender cotton for flowers, a small evergreen shrub about 75cm tall with aromatic, feathery gray-green foliage and, in summer, many small round flowerheads on slender stalks standing up above the foliage. The flowers are a pleasing pale creamy yellow, or creamy white in **'Edward Bowles'**, or primrose yellow in **'Sulphurea'**. Best grown in full sun in well-drained soils, they become leggy on soil that is too fertile. *Santolina* are good as edging for beds and herb gardens, but unfortunately flowering tends to destroy the rounded shape, and dead patches often develop. Clip off faded flowers immediately, or grow hardier *S. chamaecyparissus* (Z6–9) as a foliage plant, pruning hard in spring to prevent flower formation and to keep the plant compact; some consider losing the brassy yellow flowers an advantage.

SANTOLINA PINNATA 'SULPHUREA'

YUCCA   Z below

Yuccas are dramatic evergreens with thick, swordlike leaves that stand stiffly around a woody crown, or arch over in *Y. recurvifolia* (Z7–9) (*see p.18*). Yuccas are wonderful architectural plants as specimens or focal points in a border, or where a subtropical effect is wanted.

The leaves of *Y. filamentosa* (Z5–10) (*below*) are gray-green, edged with fine hairs. After about four years, a new crown will produce a magnificent spire of fragrant, creamy white bells standing up to 6½ft/2m high. It is easily grown in any well-drained soil in a hot position in full sun. Once established, it can easily withstand drought. It dislikes excessive winter moisture. *Y. flaccida*, with leaves that bend over at the tips, is hardy in zones 5–9. **'Ivory'** is a good flowerer; **'Golden Sword'** is smaller, with superb variegation. *Y. gloriosa* (Z7–10) is a larger plant.

YUCCA FILAMENTOSA

MORE CHOICES

Azara (see p.62)
Amelanchier canadensis (see p.66)
Berberis (see pp.46, 66)
Callistemon (see p.62)
Calluna (see p.56)
Colutea (see p.67)
Coronilla (see p.63)
Cotoneaster (see pp.56, 60)
Erica (see p.56)
Escallonia (see p.48)
Fremontodendron (see p.63)
Genista (see p.67)
Hippophae (see p.68)
Indigofera (see p.42)
Kerria (see p.42)
Pieris (see p.59)

Convolvulus cneorum (Z8–10)
A small, sun-loving semi-hardy shrub to 24in/60cm tall with narrow leaves that have a silvery, silky sheen. Throughout the summer and into autumn it is covered with a succession of trumpet-shaped white flowers, pink in bud and with a slight yellow throat. It requires well-drained soil and is ideal for the front of a hot border in association with other Mediterranean shrubs, such as lavender and rosemary. It can also be grown in a container, given protection in winter where necessary. It naturally forms a very neat, mounded shape, and no pruning should be required.

SHRUBS FOR CONTAINERS

ABUTILON 'KENTISH BELLE' (Z8–10)

Abutilon do well in pots, in a fertile soil mix in full sun. In cold climates they can be overwintered in an unheated greenhouse or may continue to flower in a conservatory. Use stakes to give support.

BERBERIS × STENOPHYLLA 'CORALLINA COMPACTA' (Z6–9)

A dwarf evergreen barberry, rounded and spiny with small yellow flowers in spring. In winter, shelter from winds and make sure that the soil mix does not get waterlogged.

CALLUNA VULGARIS 'SILVER QUEEN' (Z5–7)

A lovely heather for a pot or windowbox, with silver-gray foliage all year round and pink flowers in late summer. *Calluna* are ideal container plants, given a well-drained acidic soil mix.

CYTISUS × BEANII (Z7–8)

A low-growing, spreading, deciduous shrub that will tumble over the edges of low pots, bearing yellow flowers in early spring. Add sand to its soil mix and place in full sun. Drought-tolerant, it survives some neglect in summer.

ELAEAGNUS ANGUSTIFOLIA (Z3–8)

A beautiful medium-sized deciduous shrub with silver leaves and small, sweetly scented greenish yellow flowers in spring. Best for full sun or partial shade. Tolerates pruning to shape.

ERICA × DARLEYENSIS 'JENNY PORTER' (Z7–8)

Evergreen, winter-flowering heaths are ideal for year-round displays. They need acidic soil mix and look good as underplanting for larger acidic soil-loving shrubs such as *Pieris* or azaleas.

CAMELLIA SASANQUA 'NARUMIGATA' (Z7–8)

Very elegant, spreading, medium-sized evergreen with small, glossy leaves and single, pink-tinged white flowers carried in late winter and early spring. Must be grown in acidic soil mix and kept moist at all times. Good for shade. Protect from cold, drying winds.

CHOISYA TERNATA (Z9–10)

Handsome in a city garden, naturally forming a compact, rounded mound of glossy, lobed foliage, with clusters of small, white flowers in spring. Give it a good-sized container, in sun or shade, and feed well to maintain healthy foliage. Look for 'Sundance' if you want bright, yellow leaves.

CISTUS × DANSEREAUI 'DECUMBENS' (Z8–10)

Being drought-tolerant, rock roses are splendid container shrubs. Mix some sand into the soil mix to give them good drainage, and shelter in winter where necessary. Do not prune; if they start to look leggy, they are better planted out in the garden or replaced.

FUCHSIA 'RICCARTONII' (Z8–10)

"Hardy" fuchsias, unlike the showier tender ones, can be left in pots outdoors all year in favorable areas. In spring, prune plants cut down by cold to within 4in/10cm of the soil mix. Best in full sun.

HEBE ALBICANS (Z9–10)

An evergreen gray-leaved *Hebe* with white flowers in summer, forming a neat mound that suits the formal style. Use a sandy soil mix for good drainage, and site in full sun. Provide protection in winter.

HIBISCUS ROSA-SINENSIS (MIN. 50°F/10°C)

A pot that can be moved into a greenhouse or conservatory over winter makes it possible to grow tender hibiscus in cold climates. *H. rosa-sinensis* flowers all summer, in a wide range of colors.

HYDRANGEA MACROPHYLLA 'LANARTH WHITE' (Z6–9)

Mophead hydrangeas make ideal container plants for sun or shade, flowering in late summer. Blue flowers can be kept blue in acidic soil mix. Prune the stems down to fat new buds in spring to keep them compact.

LAVANDULA STOECHAS (Z8–9)

Lavenders make good container plants but may be short-lived. Best grown in full sun, with some sand mixed into their soil mix, but do not let them dry out. Where not hardy, move French lavender under glass for protection over winter.

PIERIS JAPONICA 'PURITY' (Z6–8)

An ideal small *Pieris* for pots, this is evergreen, with sprays of white flowers in early spring. 'Little Heath' is even smaller and will fit in a windowbox. *Pieris* need acidic soil mix and a fair amount of moisture, especially when in growth in spring.

ROSMARINUS OFFICINALIS PROSTRATUS GROUP (Z8–10)

A creeping rosemary only 6in/15cm tall that needs winter shelter in cold climates, this will grow on a cool windowsill to provide sprigs for cooking. Mix some sand into its soil mix, and keep it in a sunny position.

SENECIO CINERARIA 'SILVER DUST' (Z8–10)

A beautiful and useful foliage plant for container displays, whose gray-yellow flowers are often trimmed off. It will not survive cold winters, but is often replaced annually: small inexpensive plants bought in spring grow quickly.

SKIMMIA JAPONICA SUBSP. *REEVESIANA* (Z7–9)

Unlike other *Skimmia*, this flowers and fruits freely when grown on its own. It does best in shade, forming a neat, rounded shape. Its leaf color is best when grown in acidic soil mix. Keep out of strong winds.

POTENTILLA FRUTICOSA 'PRIMROSE BEAUTY' (Z3–7)

Potentilla fruticosa types are among the hardiest and most easily grown deciduous shrubs for containers, flowering freely through summer. They can be trimmed with shears in late winter to keep a neat habit. For full sun or partial shade.

SYRINGA MEYERI 'PALIBIN' (Z4–7)

This little lilac will grow no taller than 4–5ft/1.2–1.5m, ideal for a pot. It has small leaves and is covered in clusters of purple-pink flowers in summer. Remove spent flowerheads to encourage more flowers later in the summer.

RHODODENDRON 'VUYK'S ROSYRED' (Z6–8)

Dwarf rhododendrons and azaleas have fibrous (rather than thick, treelike) roots, which make them perfect for pot-growing. Plant in acidic soil mix in full sun or shade, and keep well fed and watered throughout the year. Deadhead for more flowers.

VIBURNUM OPULUS 'COMPACTUM' (Z4–8)

A dwarf, deciduous viburnum, with clusters of white flowers followed by red berries that are popular with birds. In autumn the leaves make a good show. A very easy and tough plant to grow in an exposed position.

MORE CHOICES

Convolvulus cneorum (see p.73)
Hypericum (see p.49)
Lavatera (see p.71)
Nandina domestica (see p.45)
Prunus triloba, P. tenella 'Fire Hill' (see p.43)
Spiraea japonica (see p.44)

More good camellias:
C. japonica (see p.46):
'Akashigata' Deep pink
'Debutante' Light pink
'Guilio Nuccio' Coral
'Lady Vansittart' White striped rose-pink
'Masayoshi' Red petals with white marbling
'Nuccio's Gem' White
'Ville de Nantes' Red with white marbling
C. × williamsii (see p.64):
'Donation' Superbly long-flowering, pink
'Francis Hanger' White
'Golden Spangles' Pink, leaves marked yellow

Other good Rhododendron:
• The R. yakushimanum hybrids named after the Seven Dwarves, e.g. 'Doc'
• Dwarf evergreens:
'Carmen' Red
'Cilipinense' White, deep pink in bud
'Purple Gem' Light purple
'Temple Belle' Pink
'Yellow Hammer' Yellow
• Evergreen azaleas:
'Apple Blossom' Pink
'Blue Danube' Violet
'Delaware Valley White'
'Hatsugiri' Crimson
'Hinode-giri' Red
'Hinomayo' Strong red
'Martha Hitchcock' White, edged magenta
'Mother's Day' Rose-red
'Palestrina' White with a faint pink eye
'Rosebud' Double pink
'Salmon Beauty' Coral

INDEX

Page numbers in *italics*
indicate illustrations.

ACKNOWLEDGMENTS

Picture research Louise Thomas
Illustrations Karen Cochrane
Index Hilary Bird

DK Publishing would like to thank:
All staff at the RHS, in particular Susanne
Mitchell, Karen Wilson, and Barbara Haynes
at Vincent Square; Candida Frith-Macdonald
for editorial assistance.

Photography
The publisher would like to thank the
following for their kind permission to
reproduce their photographs:
(key: a=above; b=below; c=center; l=left;
r=right; t=top)

Garden Picture Library: Didier Willery 66bl;
Howard Rice front cover br, back cover tl, 6,
8tr, 8b, 10bl, 11br, 19br, 38c; John Glover
17cl, 20br; J.S. Sira 9br, 77tr; Lynne Brotchie
13tr; Mayer/Le Scanff 9tl; Neil Holmes 39bl,
70bl, 72bl; Ron Evans 21tl

Garden Matters: 10br, 16br, 25tl, 76tc;
J. Feltwell 57br; John & Irene Palmer 17t,
49br; Martin P. Land 66bc; Steffie Shields
10bc
John Glover: 12tr, 18br, 22br
Jerry Harpur: 2c
Andrew Lawson: 12bl, 14bl
S & O Mathews Photography: 19t
Howard Rice: 14br, 26c
Harry Smith Collection: front cover cla,
47bc
Elizabeth Whiting & Associates:
back cover ca
Jo Whitworth: 11tl, 15tl, 15br, 23tl, 23br,
24bl, 59bl

American Horticultural Society
Visit the AHS at www.ahs.org or call them at
1-800-777-7631 ext. 10. Membership benefits
include *The American Gardener* magazine,
free admission to flower shows, the free seed
exchange, book services, and the Gardener's
Information Service.